EMOTIONAL FITNESS

changing the way you think and feel

by

Paul Bird

**Grosvenor House
Publishing Limited**

Cover designed by Enjoy Marketing

First published in Britain by
Grosvenor House Publishing in 2011
Edited by Nicki Hayes
28-30 High Street, Guildford, Surrey, GU1 3HY.
www.grosvenorhousepublishing.co.uk

A CIP record for this book
is available from the British Library

ISBN 978-1-908105-554

Emotional Fitness

Emotional Fitness is a must read for anyone who has ever wondered what drives the way we think and feel. Providing a fascinating insight into the world of human emotions it explores the science behind the emotional - rational battle which takes place in the brain resulting in so many of today's emotional problems. Using a unique model (the SEARCH), derived from the authors own coaching experiences with clients, it examines the link between human instincts, emotions and thoughts and provides a wealth of Emotional Fitness tips to help people cope with the pressures of modern living.

Disclaimer

The contents of this book represent the observations of the author and are based upon his own coaching experiences, unless otherwise stated. This book is presented for educational purposes only. It is not intended to diagnose, prescribe, treat, mitigate or cure any medical or psychological condition nor to recommend specific information, products or services as treatment of any medical or psychological conditions. The reader should be aware that the information provided herein is not intended as medical advice and should not be used as an alternative or substitute for consulting with a fully qualified medical doctor, psychologist or psychiatrist. The author makes no claim that the advice or workouts provided in this book will guarantee results as every reader's circumstances will be different and the reader alone is responsible if they choose to do anything based upon what they have read here.

Contents

Acknowledgements

Without a number of people this work would never have been completed.

I would like to thank all of the clients I have ever worked with for allowing me to enter their lives and share their troubled times. Whatever I have learned about Emotional Fitness, they taught me, not the other way around.

I would like to thank my business partner Adrian Marks and his team at Enjoy Marketing, especially Damien Obringer and Stuart Dean, for their patience and support throughout countless changes to the Emotional Fitness model. Without them, the model would never have evolved.

I would like to thank my editor and good friend Nicki Hayes for her support, encouragement and lessons in how to write. Without her, *Emotional Fitness* may have ended up in the canal at the bottom of my garden. I would also like to thank my good friend John Hardcastle for his ideas and suggestions which helped shape the content of this book in its early days.

And last but by no means least, I would like to express my gratitude, appreciation, love, and thanks to my wife Diana and my daughters Emma and Ella, without whose support I could not have dedicated the time to this project. Whatever I am today I owe to them. They will always remain the people I love more than myself, and my best friends.

Paul Bird

Foreword

"You don't get to choose how you're going to die or when. You only get to choose how you're going to live."

Joan Baez

Today, more than at any time in history, people are searching for something. For many, the ultimate target of that search is said to be achieving happiness.

What, though, is happiness?

Happiness isn't something that can be found or bought. Happiness is a transient emotion that we all feel from time to time when fully engrossed in something and enjoying the experience. Happiness is not a permanent state. Like all emotions, it can disperse as quickly as it arrives. Asking people to pursue happiness therefore, is like asking them to chase the wind.

Of course, there are things that we can do which make us feel happier for short moments:

- A refreshing drink
- A meal with friends
- An act of kindness or generosity
- A romantic encounter
- Watching our loved ones succeed
- Watching a good film, or our team win at sports ...

These, and many more similar experiences, are wonderful but they only provide us with a temporary pass into the enclosure of happiness.

John Lennon once said:

"Life is what happens to you while you're busy making other plans."

In similar vein I believe that:

"Happiness is what emerges while you're busy doing things you enjoy."

In 2005, an opinion poll carried out by GfK NOP for The Happiness Formula series on BBC television, attempted to define and measure happiness.[1] The survey showed that the proportion of people saying they were "very happy" was just 36%, down from the 52% recorded in 1957. In America too, similar surveys have found that levels of life satisfaction have gradually declined over the last twenty-five years. Clearly wealth, the Holy Grail of Western society, has failed to bring with it additional happiness.

This BBC poll included some interesting findings:

- 81% of people interviewed wanted increased happiness to be a Government goal, compared with only 13% who wanted the Government to focus on increased wealth
- 52% agreed that more emphasis should be placed on teaching children happiness rather than education aimed at preparing them for the world of work. Only 43% disagreed
- 43% said that their neighbourhood was less friendly than it was 10 years ago, compared to 22% of people who said it was friendlier

---

[1] The GfK NOP opinion poll for The Happiness Formula series was conducted by telephone. The fieldwork was carried out between 28-30 October 2005. The sample size was 1001 adults aged 15 or over, and the margin of error was +/– 3%.

- 48% said that relationships were the biggest factor in making them happy
- Only 24% said that health was what made them happy
- When asked to choose the two most important sources of happiness in their lives, only 77 people out of 1001 said work fulfilment
- It is often said that friendships are crucial to our sense of happiness, but 6 out of 10 people in this survey admitted to speaking to only five friends or fewer each week; 2 out of 10 spoke to only one or two friends; and one person in 25 talked to no friends at all
- When asked what happiness meant to them, family and friends came first, followed by contentment and inner peace
- Nearly half of the married people interviewed said they were "very happy" whereas only a quarter of single people said the same
- Of the people who described themselves as "very happy", 45% said they were in "very good" health whereas only 23% of people who described themselves as "fairly happy" said they were in very good health
- Interestingly, when asked whether they would take a legal drug to make them happy, 72% of people said no and only 26% said yes, suggesting that people want to find happiness naturally.

There is much debate over whether surveys like this are right to suggest that our overall happiness is in decline. What is clear though, is that people are searching for something more than just wealth accumulation: they want greater meaning and a better sense of balance in their lives. Increasing levels of wealth throughout the world have, undoubtedly, improved happiness, but there appears to be a point at which further increases in wealth make no significant difference to people's happiness quotas. Increased wealth often involves increased levels of work and, as this survey shows, work comes fairly low down on people's list of factors which promote happiness.

At the end of the day though we have to recognise that happiness is only one of many human emotions. The Dalai Lama once said:

"As human beings we all want to be happy and free from misery... we have learned that the key to happiness is inner peace. The greatest obstacles to inner peace are disturbing emotions such as anger, attachment, fear and suspicion, while love and compassion and a sense of universal responsibility are the sources of peace and happiness."

Dalai Lama

To search for happiness alone therefore is perhaps a little short sighted. If we are to achieve lasting happiness we need to understand and master the full range of our emotional spectrum so that we can not only enjoy the good times but also prevent ourselves being destroyed by the bad times. To suggest that somehow happiness can be achieved in isolation from our other emotions, or that we can achieve a permanent state of happiness, is to fundamentally misunderstand the role and nature of emotions. Life, as the song says, is a rollercoaster. It poses many different challenges and we need a wide range of emotions to cope with the inevitable ups and downs we experience. The real human search therefore is not a search for happiness at all. It is a search for the inner peace that comes from having the ability to choose how we think and feel.

I call that ability Emotional Fitness.

In this book you will find a proven framework designed to help you achieve greater happiness by mastering the principles of Emotional Fitness. For many years physical fitness has dominated the debate on human health but the time has now come to add Emotional Fitness to our daily exercise regime. Unless we develop our emotional, as well as our physical, muscles we will always live at the mercy of whatever life throws at us and never achieve that lasting sense of inner peace to which the Dalai Lama refers.

Enjoy!

How to use this book

This book is divided into three parts. Most people will benefit from reading each part in order, then returning to the areas that resonate most with their personal situation and emotional preferences.

Here is a brief description of what each part contains:

- **PART 1: The Philosophy** (what Emotional Fitness is and why it is so important in today's society. This Part also includes a series of tips on how to handle emotional and rational overload).
- **PART 2: The Principles and practice** (introducing the **SEARCH** Emotional Fitness model and related principles as well as workouts designed to help you develop your Emotional Fitness).
- **PART 3: The Proof** (a collection of success stories about real people who have changed their lives for the better by following the principles contained in this book).

A poem to begin

The SEARCH

If you don't want your life to be left on the shelf
You'd better start changing your view of your self
Get rid of the critic that's inside your head
Decide for yourself what you stand for instead

Don't let emotions ruin your path
Capture your worries and fears and just laugh
These are the villains who seek to protect
But demand that they show you the utmost respect

Forget all the bad things that happened to you
And start to create a more positive view
Imagine a future fulfilling your dreams
Accept it as real no matter how hard it seems

Focus on people and what you can give
But don't ever let them dictate how you live
Try not to exploit or depend upon others
See the whole world as your sisters and brothers

When criticism rages inside your head
Let words of praise come out instead
Forgive those who offend you and if you cannot
Then at least let go so your soul doesn't rot

Strive to be the best that you can
Set yourself goals and a do-able plan
Never give up when the going gets tough
Just do your best - that should be enough

And whatever you do when things go wrong
Look in the mirror and sing this song
"Que sera sera" what will be will be
but making things change - that's up to me"

Don't ever let pleasure or comfort dictate
Your desire to improve or the size of your plate
Break free from habits that are not really you
Decide for yourself what you can and can't do

Learn to let go and respect diversity
Learn to accept the law of uncertainty
Let your rules and opinions sometimes give way
To allow trust and humility adequate sway

Learn to show yourself some respect
Take time out from life to stop and reflect
Search *for the beauty in all that you view*
Give thanks and remember, " It's great to be YOU"

Paul Bird

Part 1: The Philosophy

This part of the book explores:

- The Emotional Fitness philosophy and why it is so important in today's society.
- Why choosing how we think and feel is difficult, at times
- The need for a new mindset
- The six basic human instincts (SEARCH)
- How our brain chooses how we think and feel
- The emotional : rational battle
- How to cope with emotional overwhelm
- How to cope with rational overwhelm

Chapter 1.1: Why Emotional Fitness ?

A great deal is said these days about the threat to our planet from global warming. My sense, however, is that the real challenge facing the human race is not saving the planet. The planet will survive long after we have departed. The real challenge is saving the human race itself. I truly believe that, unless we develop our Emotional Fitness, learning how to control the instincts and emotions that drive self-interest, greed, violence and an unhealthy obsession with wealth and self-gratification, the human race is destined to self-destruct.

Human evolution has brought with it incredible advances in science, medicine and technology. Yet, we continue to see our world being torn apart by emotional forces: wars justified on political, commercial, territorial and even allegedly spiritual ideologies; neighbours at war with one another over minor disputes; mob looting following temporary blackouts or natural disasters; growing gang violence and intimidation; growing domestic violence and citizens of all countries demonstrating intolerance of (and violence towards) their fellow citizens.

When I began writing this book, in England a man was gunning down 14 people in Whitehaven Cumbria whilst another was terrorising the Northeast of the country, murdering his girlfriend's new boyfriend before shooting a policemen in the face and turning the gun on himself. When I was finishing this book President Barack Obama, on January 12th 2011, addressed the American nation following the assassination attempt on Republican politician Gabrielle Giffords in Arizona, an attack which left six people dead including a nine year old child.

President Obama said:

"At a time when our discourse has become so sharply polarized — at a time when we are far too eager to lay the blame for all that ails the world at the feet of those who think differently than we do — it's important for us to pause for a moment and make sure that we are talking with each other in a way that heals, not a way that wounds."

Maybe at the time you are reading this, something similarly incomprehensible is happening where you are. And yet, whilst we ponder such tragic events, we simultaneously see incredible acts of human bravery and selflessness, demonstrating that human emotions have the potential to be both incredibly uplifting and utterly destructive. The Dali Lama once suggested that all human beings have the potential for kindness. I agree, but I believe that such potential can only be achieved if we learn to harness the basic instincts that drive our emotions.

President Obama is right. The time has come for us all to stand back and re-assess how we think, feel and behave. The brutal reality today is that when our emotions reign unchecked, they can quickly become our personal Puppet Master, pulling our strings and dictating what we do. Unless we recognise and check this trend, we risk becoming slavish victims to animal like instincts that can drive us towards obesity, alcohol and drug dependency, poisonous relationships, uncontrollable violence and other self-destructive behaviours.

During the last decade significant progress has been made in heightening awareness of the risk to public health from a lack of physical fitness. It is now time to give equal attention to our need to achieve Emotional Fitness. Consider for a moment these statistics:

- 1/5 of early deaths in the UK are related to mental health problems, compared to under 1/6 for both heart disease and cancer
- Spending on mental health services in the UK has increased by nearly 50% since 2001

- 1 in 4 people in the UK are affected by depression or anxiety at any given time and only 1/4 of these get medical help
- Stress costs UK businesses £3.7 billion each year with 13 million working days lost through stress related problems
- People reporting stress related problems in the UK lose an average of 29 working days per year.

Such statistics just keep coming, demonstrating that our mental health is under attack as never before.

Emotional Fitness therefore is a timely call for all of us to strengthen our emotional muscles so that we can survive the pressures of modern living. As the ancient Greek philosopher Epictetus once wisely observed,

"It's not what happens to you but how you react to it that matters."

To put such a philosophy into practice however we must develop our Emotional Fitness through a better understanding of :

- how the processes that control how we think, feel and behave actually work
- how we can strengthen our ability to choose how we respond to life (rather than allowing our mind to impose choice upon us).

To understand why these things are important just consider for a moment the case of Louise.

Louise came to see me suffering from stress. She had recently started to have panic attacks to the point where she felt afraid to drive or even go to work. Her mind was awash with a variety of thoughts regarding the cause of her problem and her feelings of being out of control, thoughts which were confused and unclear. Despite being a practitioner of several alternative therapies herself, Louise was struggling to cope.

Louise's life was, to put it simply, out of balance. The job she was doing was not making the most of her talents and she hated the commercial pressures she was under; her relationship with her partner was good but past relationship problems with others left her wary of long term commitment; the pressure of coping with a job she hated was making her physically ill, leaving her weak and vulnerable and she had recently had a minor car accident which had further knocked her confidence.

She was starting to doubt her own self worth and was frustrated at her inability to make decisions and overcome the emotional insecurity which was driving a disturbing sense of panic. For Louise, life had become a snowstorm. Each problem she experienced was like a snowflake, unique in its own right but indistinguishable from all the others. Combined together, these snowflakes had piled up into snow drifts around her, changing her landscape and making forward movement very difficult.

Louise's case is not untypical, in my experience, of what can happen when life gets out of control. Our thoughts and feelings take over our lives and we allow them to define who we are and what we do. We experience a terrible and often vicious mental battle in which our thoughts and feelings, far from helping us, conspire against us.

Understanding the Philosophy and Principles contained in this book helped Louise to understand why this happens. She learned to recognise that thoughts and feelings are simply by-products of our brain's activity and that we can choose not to allow them to dictate who we are and how we feel. Using the practical techniques you will find throughout this book she learned to master the physical feelings and emotions which were dominating her world and began to change the inner self talk that was adding fuel to her flames.

Louise learned to stop being afraid of her feelings and thoughts. She learned to accept them as temporary messengers communicating that she needed to make changes in her life. She began to focus on what she could do rather than being overwhelmed by thoughts of what she couldn't do. She changed her job, committed fully to the man she loved and started a new career providing alternative therapies which had always been her dream.

Louise did not become someone else. She simply restored CHOICE in her life and found her true sense of self. From that moment on she never looked back and happiness was restored in her life. To find out why so many of us react to life's problems in this and similar ways, and more importantly, to find out what we can do about it, I encourage you to read on.

Emotional Fitness is not a spiritual philosophy. It is a message of practical enlightenment based on simple techniques that I have used to help many people take emotional control of their lives. It is a timely call for a new understanding of the role emotions play in our life.

Chapter 1.2. It's a simple life

Life is a simple proposition, best summed up for me by my daughter Emma. At the age of 16, having overheard a conversation my wife and I were having about the challenges of modern life, Emma suddenly interrupted, saying:

"Dad you were born, get over it. You'll die, get used to it. You're alive now, so get on with it."

Naturally, we were somewhat taken aback at the time. I have to say though, having had time to reflect upon her observation, I find her youthful wisdom compelling. When you consider life carefully, the formula is indeed very simple. After all, we are all born, we all die and there is a 'bit in the middle'. The secret to life, therefore, must surely lie in getting the most out of that 'bit in the middle'. How to achieve such a simple goal is the big question.

Visit the Internet or any good bookstore and you will find hundreds of self help titles. You will find advice on how to be happy, get rich, be successful, find your perfect partner, win friends and influence people, boost your self confidence, lose weight, get fit, improve your health, cope with stress and depression, set goals and achieve them, achieve your dreams, and even find spiritual enlightenment. In fact the sheer volume of self-help material alone can make knowing where to start a daunting task.

Apply my daughter's simple logic though, and enjoying your 'bit in the middle' all boils down to one thing - **how you FEEL.** After all, you either feel good or you don't and if you don't, then being successful, wealthy or achieving your dreams will seem pointless.

Today, people judge their quality of life more by how they feel than by any other measure. If you ask people how they are, they don't tell you what they think, they tell you how they feel. They don't say, "I think happy", "I think great" or "I think depressed". They say, "I feel happy", "I feel great", or "I feel depressed". The simple fact is that when we feel good we don't take life too seriously or think about it too much, we just enjoy it. But when we don't feel good we take life very seriously and think far too much about it.

The secret to enjoying our 'bit in the middle', and therefore the ultimate secret to achieving happiness, lies in our ability to choose how we feel and think.

People who 'choose' how they feel and think are 'Emotionally Fit'. They live in a world of opportunity where potential is limited only by their own imagination and effort. They develop a confident 'can do' rather than a 'can't do' mentality. They react with flexibility, optimism and expectancy, which allows them to roll with life's ups and downs whilst exploiting the best in any situation.

People who can't choose how they feel and think are not 'Emotionally Fit'. They live in a world where they are slaves to emotions like worry, anxiety, frustration, desire and self-doubt. They become dependent upon other people and external events. They see limited choices and feel trapped, stressed, or depressed. They develop a 'can't do' rather than a 'can do' mentality and they blame themselves, others or external forces for their predicament, seeing life as a burden.

Which world do you live in?

If you live in the emotionally unfit world and currently feel unhappy, depressed, lost, anxious, stressed or worried then do yourself a favour right now.

Stop beating yourself up!

You are not unusual, defective, missing something, lacking in some way or, indeed, alone. Millions of people throughout the world are finding it hard to enjoy their 'bit in the middle' because of the pressures of modern living. The biggest drain on people's mental health today however, is the common misconception that changing the way they feel and think is dependent on external factors changing. The good news is that, whatever situation you are currently in, you can transform your life by choosing to take control of how you feel and think rather than relying on factors you cannot control. In other words, **you can choose to become 'Emotionally Fit'.**

Achieving Emotional Fitness however, doesn't guarantee that there won't be times when you feel unhappy or experience emotional pain or mental conflict. Indeed you are supposed to feel these things because they are part of being human. We need pain at times to aid our survival. Pain alerts us to danger, tells us when we are heading in the wrong direction and even motivates us to change. What being Emotionally Fit means, as my daughter suggests, is having the ability to choose how we think and feel, even when our life spirals out of control.

Life's spirals

Choosing how we think and feel is important because life is like the weather, unpredictable.

Sometimes we enjoy upward spirals, when everything works out exactly as we planned it. These are the times when:

- We relax and forget about daily chores and responsibilities
- We fall in love with someone or something
- We enjoy new experiences
- We become so engrossed in what we are doing that time flies by unnoticed.

In upward spirals like these, analysing and questioning our life is the last thing on our mind. We simply enjoy our 'bit in the middle' without really thinking about it, and that's how it should be. In my work as a hypnotherapist and coach I can safely say that I have never been approached by anyone complaining about their upward spirals and asking me to turn them down a little.

At other times though, we experience downward spirals, when events seem to conspire against us and everything that could go wrong does. These are the times when:

- Everything we touch breaks
- Every bill imaginable flies through the letterbox
- Everybody we ring puts us on hold
- Every road we drive down has a traffic jam
- Our computer says "bye" just before we press "save"
- We stand in line at the bank and the person in front of us pays in their weekly takings, in coins
- We reach the office and realise that we've left the report we spent all night working on at home
- Personal setbacks, such as illness, death, redundancy, and relationship breakdown, wreak havoc in our life
- Or external events, like those in New York on 9/11, or the Arizona shootings I mentioned earlier, blow us off course into feelings of anger or despair.

In downward spirals, like these, our 'bit in the middle' can feel anything but enjoyable. We start analysing and questioning our life, desperately searching for answers, meaning and a way back towards an upward spiral. And today, the potential for such negative spirals has never been greater due to:

- The sheer pace of life
- The incessant emphasis on material possession, success and image

- The demand for instant gratification
- Increasing dependency on mechanisation and technology
- The proliferation and immediacy of modern communication
- The changing nature of work
- The demand for greater efficiency from fewer workers
- The threat of redundancy
- The breakdown of family structures
- Population growth resulting in more and more people occupying less and less space
- The integration within most societies of different cultures
- Increasing disenchantment with religious and spiritual dogma.

And strangely enough, even achieving success, the Holy Grail of western society, offers no respite. How many times have you seen top sports men and women, business leaders and celebrities, achieve career and financial success yet struggle with negative emotions that destroy their lives? People like Tiger Woods, Marcus Trescothick, Frank Bruno, Brian Moore, George Michael, Britney Spears and many, many more. Their struggle had nothing to do with a lack of physical fitness, self-belief, personal goals or wealth, the mantra of many self-help books. They were simply victims of a much more common and deeper problem: self-destructive emotions that promote self-destructive behaviour.

Despite all of these challenges however, which are likely to increase rather than decrease in the future, the good news is that my daughter's simple words still ring true. In downward spirals we either cope with what life throws at us, what my daughter called 'get on with it', or we become one of life's victims. Emotional Fitness is about choosing to 'get on with it'.

The power of choice

One of the problems I often come across with my clients however, is that choosing how they feel and think is difficult for them because they allow how they feel and what they think to define who they are. I point out to them that how they feel and think is **NOT** who they are. By far and away the most important message Emotional Fitness has to convey is this:

Feelings and thoughts are by-products of your brain's activity. You are much more than both of these things. You are the driving force behind them and you can take control of them any time YOU CHOOSE TO.

You see, choice is one of the most underrated and yet important mental tools that we possess. We all have the ability to choose how we feel and what we think if we pay attention, but the fact is that we rarely pay attention because we are so busy going through life on autopilot. On my seminars I encourage people to become more aware of this problem using the analogy of ancient Troy.

The ancient Trojans remained safe behind the walls of their great city and the invading Greek army was unable to penetrate those walls despite months of trying. Then the Trojans became careless. They thought that the Greeks had given up and gone home, leaving behind a gigantic wooden horse, which, they assumed, was an item of worship hastily discarded in the Greek retreat. Opening their gates, they pulled the horse within the city walls to celebrate their victory. The rest is history. The horse was full of Greek soldiers who sneaked out in the dead of night and opened up the gates, allowing their comrades to storm in and ransack the city.

How is this relevant? Well your life is like the ancient city of Troy. If you pay attention to managing your thoughts and feelings, then resisting life's downward spirals is much easier, no matter how fierce the attack. But, if you become careless, let down your guard, and allow negative thoughts and feelings to ransack your mental city whenever they like then, before you know where you are, you will have surrendered control of your life.

In modern computer language we use the term Trojans to describe viruses that sneak into our operating system and corrupt its performance. Thoughts and feelings can be just like those viruses. Thoughts and feelings may seem harmless enough, just like the Trojan horse, but take your eye off them and they can combine to create a force as destructive as any Greek army or modern computer virus. Emotional Fitness is about choosing the feelings and thoughts that you allow into your city.

Thoughts v feelings

To choose how we feel and think we first need to understand exactly what choice is. Choice is our ability to evaluate information, review different options, solve problems and make decisions. Choice involves a partnership between the rational (thinking) and emotional (feeling) parts of our brain, something we will explore in more detail in the next chapter.

When it comes to Emotional Fitness though, which is more important: how we feel or how we think? Supporters of positive thinking have long suggested that thoughts are more important because they change the way we feel. To test this theory I invite you to try this exercise (please commit to this fully, don't allow your thoughts to tell you that you don't need to do it).

The Thoughts v Feelings Challenge

Read the text in italics and then carry out the exercise:

Recall a time in your life when everything was going great for you, when you were totally happy and having fun. Close your eyes for a few moments and recall that experience in as much detail as you can. Notice what you see, hear, feel and sense, as if you were back there reliving that exact moment. Do whatever you need to do to make this experience as real as possible and stay with it until it starts to fade.

Do this now and open your eyes when you have finished.

What physical feelings are you experiencing in your body now?
What emotions are you experiencing?
What thoughts are going through your mind?

If you committed fully to this exercise you will have, at least partially, re-experienced some of the joy of that moment in your life and your feelings and thoughts will have changed from where they were when you started the exercise.

This simple exercise demonstrates that, by focusing your thoughts on positive events, you CAN influence how you feel. The universal 'Law of Attraction', extensively featured in Rhonda Byrne's book *The Secret*, takes this a stage further by suggesting that what you think about actually determines what you attract in your life. If you focus on problems (past, present or future), what you don't want, or negative ideas, then you give off a negative energy, which attracts more of the same. In other words you attract more problems, more of what you don't want and more negativity in your life. On the other hand, if you focus on what you do want, positive outcomes, and you expect and visualise success, then you give off a positive energy, which attracts the very things you do want.

The Law of Attraction has great merit and there is no doubt in my mind that by developing such a positive and focussed mindset you can motivate yourself to achieve great things. Motivational messages like the Law of Attraction are undoubtedly inspirational, but we must not lose sight of two very real considerations:

1. Anyone who has ever been successful at anything had to take action.

Visualising our future, thinking about and imagining success is all well and good but we also need to take action in order to make anything happen. Even lottery winners have to buy a ticket. People who claim to have used the Law of Attraction as the basis of their success don't always tell you how much hard work and effort went in to being in the right place at the right time and how many times they had to cope with rejection before they were successful.

The Law of Attraction coupled with action is what actually makes people successful.

2. Choosing how we feel and think is easy in an upward spiral. When we hit a downward spiral, however, our thinking and feelings can turn stubbornly resistant to such a positive outlook.

This point is vital in the context of understanding Emotional Fitness. The problem with positive thinking is that it implies that we just need to change our thoughts and everything will slot into place. But as anyone who has suffered with stress, anxiety, worry, panic attacks or other mental health problems will tell you, there are times when this seems impossible.

In my work as a hypnotherapist and coach, I have worked with many people who have reached a point in their life where their negative thoughts and feelings drown out any attempts to change. Now, these were not stupid people, they were intelligent and they knew that they needed to change the way they were thinking and feeling, but they found making that change very difficult. Even successful athletes like Tiger Woods, for whom setting goals and visualising positive outcomes is second nature in their chosen sport, have found that changing their thoughts and feelings can prove difficult in downward spirals.

The problem is that choosing to think and feel positive can sometimes seem impossible when we hit a downward spiral, especially one that threatens our sense of security or wellbeing. When this happens our survival instincts take over and within fractions of a second our feelings change before we have a chance to understand, let alone come to terms with, what is happening.

Let's consider a real life example. Imagine that you suddenly receive a phone call to say that your child or partner has been rushed into hospital. In such circumstances you face a battle to stop yourself panicking to the point where your thinking becomes negative and irrational. And even when the initial shock of such a downward spiral has passed, thoughts regarding how you will cope or what might happen next can remain, keeping your thoughts focussed on negative outcomes. People telling you to think positively, at times like these, can be like showing a red rag to a bull.

Emotional Fitness, therefore, is not simply about thinking positively. It is about understanding and controlling our thoughts and feelings and most importantly the relationship between them, especially in downward spirals. Sometimes life is tough, hard work and painful and we have to find the inner strength to confront the brutal reality of our life before we can even begin to think or feel more positive.

The reality is that our thoughts and feelings are actually two sides of the same coin. Both are capable of leading or following the other and in the next chapter we will explore how that relationship works and why moving from negative to positive thinking can be so difficult in the face of downward spirals. The Law of Attraction is right to suggest that our thoughts can change the way we feel, but it is also true that sometimes our feelings can lock us into negative thinking. We have to recognise therefore, that our feelings and thoughts are capable of taking us to the heights of ecstasy and the depths of despair. Mastering them both through the power of choice is the only way to achieve Emotional Fitness and lasting happiness.

A new mindset

The first choice we must make therefore is to adopt a new mindset. We need to take ownership of our thoughts and feelings and declare war on the victim mentality that is engulfing our society, driving an obsession with instant solutions which involve no ownership, effort or responsibility on our part. Just take a moment to reflect on the increasing demand these days for easy solutions; pills to take away the pain of depression; pills to remove stress; gastric bands to stop hunger pangs; liposuction to remove fat; hypnotherapy to stop smoking; therapy to resolve personal issues; alcohol or drugs to take away or numb the pain of life; relentless relationship roaming to cure loneliness. Unless we stand up and take ownership of our own reality, no matter how brutal it may be, we will choose to see ourselves as the victims of external forces, rather than masters of our own destiny.

Ironically, much of the self-help market, whilst well intentioned, actually encourages this victim mentality. How many times do you see adverts on the Internet asking questions that go to the heart of people's pain?

- "Do you suffer from depression?"
- "Do you struggle to find that special relationship?"
- "Do you have money worries?"
- "Do you suffer from self doubt or lack of confidence?"
- "Do you suffer from anxiety?"

Naturally people get drawn in, thinking, "Yes I suffer from those problems, can you save me?" Once inside they are offered the miracle secrets or solutions that will change their life, only to discover that they don't (the medicine man who used to roll into town in the old westerns selling miracle cures, hair restorer and other remedies is alive and well and living in the Internet). Such adverts pray on people's negative belief that they are in some way defective or lacking something and that they need a magical solution. Every time they find something new they buy it in the hope that it will be the missing piece of their personal jigsaw.

Where Emotional Fitness differs is in its focus on one clear message:

... you already have all the resources you need.

Let me repeat that!

... you already have all the resources you need.

Emotional Fitness will help you: but not by focusing on what you don't know, by focusing on what you do know; not by encouraging you to change but by encouraging you to use the skills and talent you already have.

Emotional Fitness will help you to recognise and cope when your thoughts and feelings overwhelm you so that you can keep making choices even in downward spirals. Everything else that you need you already have. You know your strengths, limitations, talents and potential. You know the good and bad parts of your life so far. You know what's good in your life right now and what needs changing. You know the problems you face and the options you have. When your thoughts and feelings conspire against you though, you can lose sight of all of this, ending up in a confused and vulnerable victim state. In my experience when people stop allowing their lives to be dominated by negative thoughts and feelings, they soon find that positive alternatives arrive to fill the void. Accepting this is probably the biggest challenge people face in downward spirals but sometimes we have to believe in a better future even though it is not in sight.

Emotional Fitness is not a magic solution with easy answers. Developing an emotionally fit mindset is simple but it is also tough. It involves facing up to the fact that life can be brutal at times and there are no magic solutions. It means accepting that hard work, effort, and even emotional or physical pain might be involved in escaping from downward spirals. Above all though, it means taking ownership of the choices we make.

The case of Anne sums this up perfectly.

Anne came to see me suffering from claustrophobia. She had refused to enter a lift for 15 years and was afraid of confined spaces, especially the back seat of a car. Hypnotherapy revealed little in the way reasons why Anne suffered such a condition as there appeared to be no obvious incident in her life which would have triggered such a phobic response.

From the outset it became clear though that Anne was emotionally attached to her claustrophobia. It dominated her life and her thoughts and feelings convinced her that she was suffering from an "affliction" over which she had no control. Even the name "claustrophobia" gave her problem an identity and logic. I asked Anne to "do claustrophobia" in front of me. She looked at me as if I had gone mad and said she couldn't possibly reproduce it on demand, she needed to be in a lift. I suggested to her that claustrophobia did not exist. It was not something you could catch or be injected with and that she could create it at will. For a few moments she denied this and fought the idea so I asked her to close her eyes and relax.

As she did this I asked her to recall somewhere she knew well that had a lift. She began to describe her place of work. I asked her to imagine she was at work and gradually got her to imagine she was approaching the lift there. As she described this imaginary experience her demeanour changed. She became anxious, shifting her position and started to shake. As I pushed her to imagine entering the lift, tears began to roll down her cheeks as she exclaimed that she could not do it. Immediately I asked her to open her eyes and enthusiastically praised her for creating claustrophobia on demand, in my office. Her face was a picture. She looked confused and bewildered.

This may sound cruel, but the point here is that, for the first time in her life, Anne realised that claustrophobia was something she was creating in her own mind through her thoughts and feelings. Once she realised that she could influence her own thoughts and feelings, she began to slowly believe that she might be able to take ownership of her mind rather than believing she was the victim of something outside of her control.

Over the next few sessions I visited real lifts with Anne and, by distracting her thought patterns at key moments, for example when the lift doors opened, she was able to enter the lift and travel to the top. Make no mistake, this wasn't easy for Anne at first because she still experienced the physical sensations of anxiety. But, because she accepted that those feelings were not going to kill her and by distracting her thoughts, her anxiety was considerably less than she had experienced in similar situations in the past. After only a few sessions with Anne, despite not being able to enter a lift for 15 years, she raised £150 for charity in one month by undertaking 150 lift rides sponsored at £1 a trip by her friends.

What Anne's case demonstrates is that sometimes our brain locks us into the belief that we are what we feel and think but nothing could be further from the truth. We have the ability to choose and change how we feel and think but the first step often requires that we fight feelings and thoughts which seek to define and imprison us.

Emotional Fitness encourages you to accept yourself as you are but also to believe that you can do and be anything that is within your physical and mental capability. A lot of self help books rightly promote the idea of self belief but how do we achieve it ? Self belief requires ONLY that we CHOOSE to take control of our thoughts and feelings. When we doubt ourselves we do so by choosing to think about what we haven't got and what we don't know which emotionally makes us feel that we CAN'T do things. To believe in ourselves we can choose to ignore self doubt and think about what we have got and what we do know, which emotionally makes us feel that we CAN do things. So from this point forward, I encourage you to start CHOOSING to:

- **STOP** focusing on what you don't know and **START** focusing on what you do know
- **STOP** focusing on what you can't do and **START** focusing on what you can do
- **STOP** focusing on what you haven't got and **START** celebrating what you have got.
- **STOP** focussing on problems in your life and **START** looking for opportunities and solutions
- **STOP** analysing your life and **START** living it
- **STOP** talking to yourself and **START** talking to people who can help you
- **STOP** looking for solutions that somebody else has and **START** focusing on solutions that you have within you
- **STOP** procrastinating and **START** taking action
- **STOP** thinking you need to plan everything and **START** looking for opportunities (nobody who ever achieved success did so by taking the exact path they intended, they were always ambushed by opportunities)
- **STOP** walking past opportunities and **START** taking them.

In PART 2 of this book you will find a number of workouts and STOP / START exercises which, if practiced, will help you to

strengthen your Emotional Fitness and access the potential you have for lasting happiness.

Key learning points

In this chapter we have explored the need for Emotional Fitness. Here's a quick reminder of the key points.

1. Life is simple and the secret to enjoying it and finding happiness lies in **CHOOSING** how you feel and what you think.
2. Life comprises upward and downward spirals and choosing is much harder in downward spirals, due to the pressures of modern living.
3. Choice involves a complex battle between the emotional (feeling) and rational (thinking) parts of your brain. Positive thinking can help, to a point, but in downward spirals your feelings can lock you into negative thinking.
4. Emotional Fitness is the ability to "choose" how you feel and what you think even in downward spirals.
5. People who can "choose" how they think and feel are Emotionally Fit. They live in a world of opportunity where potential is limited only by their own imagination and effort. They develop a confident "can do" mentality. They react with flexibility, optimism and action. This allows them to roll with life's spirals, exploiting the best in any situation.
6. People who can't choose how they think and feel are not Emotionally Fit. They live in a world where they are slaves to emotions like worry, anxiety, frustration, desire and self-doubt. They become dependent upon other people and external events. They see limited choices and feel trapped, stressed, or depressed. They develop a "can't do" mentality and often blame themselves, others or external forces for their predicament. They see life as a burden and become its victims.

7. Achieving Emotional Fitness requires a new mindset, one that rejects the idea that we are victims of our feelings and thoughts and accepts that changing these is always possible.

In the next chapter we will explore:

- The science behind choice
- How our brain creates our feelings and thoughts
- How we make choices
- Why the rational and emotional parts of our brain do battle
- How and why people's emotional reactions differ.

Chapter 1.3: The science of choice

In the last chapter we discussed the importance of choice in achieving Emotional Fitness. In downward spirals especially, we need to choose how we feel and think to prevent our emotions and thoughts running out of control. Now, some of you are probably thinking:

"Sounds simple in theory, but exercising choice in real life is not that simple."

It can be.

Let me repeat that ...

It can be.

To understand how we can achieve this, however, we need first to understand the science behind how our brain chooses our feelings and thoughts.

If you are thinking, *"Why bother?"* then please allow me to explain.

Understanding how and why the brain creates thoughts and feelings benefits my clients by helping them to realise that they are not going crazy when they feel overwhelmed by Emotional Fitness problems like stress, depression, worry and anxiety. This understanding often provides a powerful motivator for them to reach what I call an MOD, a "Moment Of Determination". In that moment they say to themselves, "I'm better than this," and refuse to allow their brain, like some sort of Puppet Master, to dictate how they think and feel. The mental battle which we all experience between our thoughts and our feelings, especially challenging during life's downwards spirals, is the root cause of so many of today's Emotional Fitness problems. Understanding how and why that battle exists and what can be done about it is what Emotional Fitness is all about. So, where does it all start?

The role of instincts

Our journey to understand choice starts with the recognition that everything we do is driven by ancient instincts. I use the word 'driven' because instincts are hard wired into the deepest subconscious levels of our brain, reacting without us having to even think about it. They have developed over thousands of years of evolution and act as a sort of personal compass, identifying and reacting to our most basic needs.

If you want an immediate idea of what I'm talking about you only have to remember the last time you jumped out your skin when someone startled you. A sudden noise or movement can trigger our survival instinct, and before we realise what is happening we find ourselves taking evasive action. Welcome to the world of instincts.

Instincts are the foundation of our sense of searching for something. The fact is, we are always searching, not just for happiness, but for the satisfaction of our instinctive needs.

The challenge we face with Emotional Fitness is to make sure that our automatic response to our instinctive needs does not generate behaviours which are no longer appropriate in a modern society. The bloody 'kill or be killed' instincts which served our ancestors so well thousands of years ago have no place in a civilised society. The daily world news however bears testimony to the fact that we still have a long way to go before we can claim to have tamed the more savage and selfish aspects of our ancient instincts.

So how do instincts work?

Using our senses of sight, hearing, smell, taste, touch and feeling, our brain instinctively scans incoming signals from the world around us to assess our needs. When it identifies a need it triggers emotions and thoughts in our brain, which help us to work out how best to satisfy that need. Not all of our instincts are the same however. Different instincts identify different needs and trigger different emotions to guide us. The instincts that most directly affect our Emotional Fitness are what I call the SEARCH instincts, as shown in diagram 1.

Diagram 1

The SEARCH instincts

The SEARCH model

Here's what our SEARCH instincts do for us:

- Our **Survival** instinct looks after our need for physical and psychological survival
- Our **Engagement** instinct looks after our need to connect with others
- Our **Achievement** instinct looks after our need to fulfil our potential
- Our **Reward** instinct looks after our need to satisfy our needs
- Our **Control** instinct looks after our need for security
- Our **Harmony** instinct looks after our need for balance and well-being.

If these needs are satisfied, then we stand an excellent chance of enjoying our 'bit in the middle' and achieving happiness. If they are not satisfied however we can quickly become emotionally unbalanced. The key to Emotional Fitness therefore is being able to find positive ways to satisfy these instinctive needs rather than allowing them to automatically dictate how we think, feel and behave.

To identify our needs however, our brain has to be able to both 'feel' incoming signals from our senses, so that we can sense whether we 'feel' good or bad about them, and also to 'analyse' them, so that we can understand them and decide how best to satisfy them. Feeling those signals is controlled by the emotional part of our brain and analysing them is controlled by the rational part of our brain. The relationship between these two parts of the brain is actually what determines our ability to choose. Now, I realise that not all of you are science fans, and this is not a science book, so the descriptions used here will be kept short. For those of you who are interested, I have included more technical details as numbered notes in the body of the text and referenced them at the bottom of each page.

The emotional brain

The emotional part of our brain 'feels' our needs and these needs fall into two camps:

1. **Physical needs,** which include our need for air, food, water, sleep, warmth, security, and sex.
2. **Psychological needs,** which include our need to feel loved, to feel good about ourselves, to feel satisfied with who we are and to feel fulfilled by what we do.

The emotional part of our brain receives signals from our senses and scans them for signs of these physical and psychological needs. If it senses a need we experience an emotional desire to satisfy that need and a chemical[2] is sent to the front of our brain to stimulate the rational part of our brain to think about ways of satisfying that need. Once the need is satisfied another chemical[3] is released which restores us back to a satisfied state. This creates a virtuous circle, allowing us to feel our needs and then satisfy them. For example, when we are hungry (physical need) our emotional brain creates a desire for food (emotion) which motivates our rational brain to decide what to eat. Similarly, when we are lonely (psychological need) we experience a desire to engage with others (emotion) which motivates us to make contact with people. The reason we have physical needs is fairly obvious: we need to stay alive. But why do we have psychological needs?

Our psychological needs emanate from our unique sense of self-awareness, our sense of self. This sense of self is what

---

[2] An area of the brain known as the Ventral Tegmental Area (VTA) evaluates our emotional needs. When the VTA identifies needs it stimulates the Nucleus Accumbens, which fires the natural brain chemical dopamine into the front part of our brain to stimulate a rational response.

[3] Seratonin is the natural brain chemical that calms us down.

differentiates us from most animals. It provides us with a sense of our own mortality and also the ability to understand how we feel about ourselves and what we do. Someone once said, "The pig does not sit in the sty dreaming of becoming a horse" and I am pretty sure that my dog does not sit in the corner wondering whether he could have done more with his life. Humans, however, do possess a unique sense of their own existence, which allows them to think about (and make judgements about) themselves and their behaviour.

Why we have developed this sense of self is the subject of much debate. My theory is that it has evolved as a by product of the development of human language over thousands of years. As the human brain evolved we developed the ability to communicate complex thoughts, feelings and ideas (rather than just primitive animal-like grunts). From an evolutionary standpoint that allowed us to spread knowledge thereby enhancing our survival prospects. In history this marked the move from the warrior era to the wizard era as societies developed complex social structures where politics and trade became as important as the sword. This development of language would have enabled us to not only communicate our own ideas but also to receive personal feedback from others. That feedback would in turn have required us to develop an ability to self reflect. After all, if someone tells you what they think of you, you need to be able to reflect on that information and decide what to do with it.

This may sound like conjecture but there is actually a part of our emotional brain [4] which lights up when we self-reflect. This is the part of the brain which lights up when we experience emotions like love, hate, lust, disgust, contempt, pride, humiliation, gratitude, resentment, guilt, embarrassment,

---

[4] The Insula forms part of the VTA referred to in the earlier footnote. It reacts when we focus on how we feel about our sense of self.

empathy, trust, distrust, rejection and even an understanding of right and wrong - all emotions relating to how we feel about ourselves. This area of our brain appears to act as a sort of conscience, evaluating how we feel about ourselves in the light of our experiences. Developing a positive sense of self is therefore key to achieving Emotional Fitness because without that our brain will be more prone to negative self-reflection and self-doubt rather than self-confidence.

Feelings v emotions

One important thing to note is that there are two different ways in which we 'feel' our needs – physical feelings and emotions. Many people use these two terms to describe the same thing but there they are very different.

- First we experience **physical feelings.** For example, when we are hungry we 'feel' that hunger, through our stomach rumbling. When we see someone we think is attractive, we 'feel' excited, through our heart skipping a beat. Similarly, when we are rejected we 'feel' hurt, through heaviness in our chest, tightness of breath or tension in our muscles.
- Second we experience **emotions.** Emotions are not physical feelings, although they are closely linked with them. When our instincts identify our needs they trigger emotions to guide us towards or away from things in order to satisfy our needs. For example, when we experience a rumbling in our stomach, we also experience a sense of desire (emotion), which guides us towards food. When we are threatened or failing at something we experience a sense of fear (emotion), which guides us to run away or fight.

Understanding the links and differences between physical feelings and emotions is an essential part of achieving

Emotional Fitness because they need to be managed differently. Physical feelings can be controlled through breathing and relaxation techniques (after all, no one can be tense and relaxed at the same time) but emotions are more complex and the directional message they convey needs to be understood before we allow them to influence our thinking, something we shall explore in more detail in Part 2.

Unfortunately many people assume that their physical feelings, emotions, and the thoughts accompanying them represent who they are, their sense of self. The good news however, is that this is not the case. As we shall discuss later, our feelings, emotions and thoughts can be managed in a way that helps us to find out who we really are rather than what our instincts have conditioned us to become.

'Towards' and 'Away' emotions

So how does this relationship between instincts and emotions work and why do we experience such a variety of different emotions? When we receive incoming signals from our senses, we instinctively generate either 'towards' emotions, which attempt to satisfy our needs by moving us towards things, or 'away' emotions, which attempt to satisfy our needs by moving us away from things. To demonstrate this, the SEARCH model that you saw earlier can be extended to show how 'towards' emotions (upward arrows) and 'away' emotions (downward arrows) relate to our SEARCH instincts (see diagram 2).

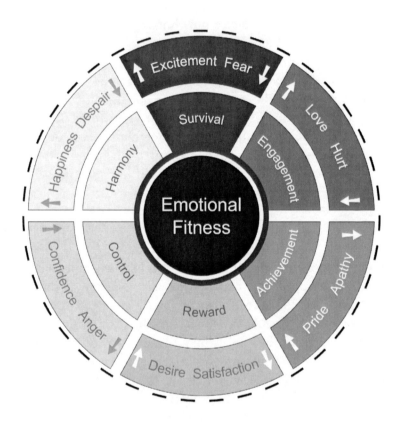

Diagram 2

The SEARCH instincts and emotions

This explanation may help to clarify this link between instincts and emotions.

- Our **Survival** instinct exists to look after our physical and psychological survival. If we 'feel' good about threats to our survival, for example when we experience the thrill of pushing ourselves beyond our comfort zone, we experience the 'towards' emotion of **Excitement**, guiding us to embrace danger or risk. If we 'feel' that such threats pose danger however, we experience the 'away' emotion of **Fear**, guiding us away from danger.
- Our **Engagement** instinct looks after our need to connect with others. If we 'feel' good about engaging with others, for example when we are attracted to someone, we experience the 'towards' emotion of **Love** which guides us towards people. If we disengage however, for example when we lose a loved one, or when someone lets us down, we experience the 'away' emotion of **Hurt**, which guides us away from people in order to protect ourselves from the pain of separation.
- Our **Achievement** instinct looks after our need to fulfil our potential. If we 'feel' good about the path our life is taking and sense that our potential is being fulfilled, we experience the 'towards' emotion of **Pride** which guides us towards our goals. But if we 'feel' bad about our direction, lost or too focused on achieving things, which add no real value to our life, we experience the 'away' emotion of **Apathy** which tries to protect us by minimising the importance of achievement.
- Our **Reward** instinct looks after our need to satisfy our needs by associating pain with unsatisfied needs and pleasure with satisfied needs. When our needs are not met we experience pain and the 'towards' emotion of **Desire** motivates us to seek satisfaction. When our needs are met we feel pleasure and the 'away' emotion of **Satisfaction**

reduces our desire and guides us away from the target of our desire.

- Our **Control** instinct looks after our need for security so that we can defend ourselves and our possessions. If we 'feel' in control we feel good about ourselves and experience the 'towards' emotion of **Confidence** which motivates us to stand up for and protect ourselves. If we 'feel' that we are losing control however we experience the 'away' emotion of **Anger**, which motivates us to defend ourselves and seize back control.

- Finally, our **Harmony** instinct looks after our need to achieve physical and psychological balance. If we feel good about our life, we experience the 'towards' emotion of **Happiness** which provides us with a sense of wellbeing. If we 'feel' bad about our life we experience the 'away' emotion of **Despair**, which alerts us to the fact that we are out of balance and need to make changes in our life.

Now, you may be thinking that there are many more words used to describe emotions that are not included here and you are right. The emotions listed here simply represent the possible ends of a spectrum in each case. A more comprehensive summary might look something like table 1.

Instinct	End of the spectrum 'towards'	Emotions in between	End of the spectrum 'away'
Survival	Excitement	Thrill, Astonishment, Anticipation, Surprise, Relief, Nervousness, Worry, Anxiety, Stress, Shock, Fright, Panic, Unease, Tenseness	Fear
Engagement	Love	Infatuation, Affection, Empathy, Sympathy, Pity, Sadness, Disgust, Liking, Disliking, Fondness, Compassion, Caring, Revulsion, Contempt, Anguish, Isolation, Embarrassment, Grief, Sorrow	Hurt
Achievement	Pride	Pride, Jealousy, Envy, Greed, Disappointment	Apathy
Reward	Desire	Pain, Irritation, Impulsiveness, Exasperation, Frustration, Longing, Suffering, Pleasure	Satisfaction
Control	Confidence	Trust, Revenge, Aggression, Rage, Insecurity, Impatience, Annoyance, Apprehension, Resentment, Bitterness	Anger
Harmony	Happiness	Ecstasy, Euphoria, Joy, Contentment, Gladness, Optimism, Hope, Remorse, Regret, Shame, Guilt	Despair

Table 1 : The range of emotions

The nature of emotions

Whatever words we use to describe our emotions however, the common mistake people make when trying to understand them is interpreting 'towards' emotions as good and 'away' emotions as bad. In reality both types of emotions can be good or bad, dependent upon the circumstances. Love, for example, sounds good but I once saw a woman feeding her 70 stone husband pizzas because she said she loved him so much she could not refuse him. On the other hand, despair sounds bad but many people have turned their lives around by reaching a point of despair. Satisfaction sounds good, but too much satisfaction can lead to laziness and addictive habits.

The important thing to remember is that emotions are only messengers. They are part of our internal compass, guiding us in the direction that best serves our needs. They should be treated as trusted advisors but like all advisors, we should understand their motivation before we accept their advice. You see there is a fundamental problem with emotions. They are short term in their focus and the *immediate* satisfaction of our needs in the fastest possible time, regardless of the long-term consequences, is their goal.

Think about it for a moment.

- When we feel hungry we want food NOW!
- When we feel sad we want cheering up NOW!
- When we feel excited we want to do something NOW!

Waiting for our needs to be satisfied leads to frustration and anxiety (try not eating for a couple of days and you will see what I mean). This short-term bias causes problems because some of our needs, especially our psychological needs, cannot always be instantly satisfied. In such cases, our emotions can overwhelm our rational thinking and guide us towards alternative sources of satisfaction, just to relieve our sense of need (sometimes with devastating consequences).

Consider this example.

Imagine that you suddenly lose your job. You might experience physical feelings like tension in your chest and a churning in your stomach. You might then experience emotions like anxiety and worry, which create an inner sense of guiding you away from the danger. Both types of reaction carry a helpful message that you need to find another job in order to survive. But in cases like this there may be no immediate solution or rational quick fix. Your emotions may therefore demand quicker satisfaction of your need and guide you towards alternative sources of satisfaction and pleasure like eating, drinking, drugs or sex. This can lead to you becoming addicted to negative habits designed to provide short-term relief.

So why is it that our emotions are so short term focused?

The reason is that, in order to monitor our physical and psychological needs, the emotional part of the brain operates outside of our conscious awareness at what we call the subconscious level. Our subconscious mind controls our life support functions like breathing, swallowing, digestion, blood circulation, temperature control and all of our internal bodily functions including brain activity. As a result it operates on a present moment basis. It focuses on breathing NOW, blinking NOW, pumping blood NOW and so on, because that is how your body functions, from one second to the next. Imagine if you had to consciously remember to breathe. I don't know about you but I lose my keys at least twice a week, if I had to remember to breathe I would die within minutes.

The emotional brain operates on the same subconscious level, allowing us to permanently monitor our needs without thinking about it. The problem is that our subconscious mind does not deal in thinking, rational argument, analysis or consideration of things like the past or the future. It relies on direction from our rational mind for that, as we shall explore in a moment. The primary focus of our subconscious brain is our survival. Its function is to instinctively identify and react to our needs in present time, which is why I describe emotional needs as short term.

Our subconscious mind is a slave to our needs, which is both good news and bad news. The good news is that it reacts instinctively to our needs. But there are two pieces of bad news.

The first is that our subconscious brain acts much faster than our conscious rational brain. By way of example, consider the 2009 BBC Television documentary, Horizon, which featured a BBC reporter undergoing tests at a prominent UK University. Placed in a brain scanner, scientists asked the reporter a series of questions whilst monitoring the electrical activity in his brain. They were eventually able to predict, by watching his brain light up, what answers he would give to any question anything up to 9 seconds before he was consciously aware of his own answers. This demonstrates that our subconscious brain takes in information and processes it so fast that our conscious mind is always playing catch up. This is why we sometimes act first and think later, "Why did I do that". Whilst our subconscious brain can respond to our thinking it can also identify our needs faster than our rational brain can keep up. This is why we sometimes find it difficult to think our way out of emotional problems, because our conscious mind does not fully understand what triggered our emotions in the first place.

The second piece of bad news is that our subconscious mind will resist any attempts to change behaviours that it senses will cause us pain or discomfort. Take the example of long term smokers. Smokers are consciously aware of the dangers of smoking but they smoke anyway. Why? Consciously they know that smoking is dangerous and they may even decide to stop, but subconsciously their brain associates smoking with relaxation, calm, looking cool, or an excuse for a well-earned break. As a result it resists the idea of stopping. When our subconscious mind interprets anything we do as pleasurable it will automatically interpret stopping it as painful, resisting and even overriding any conscious rational commitment. This is why adverts often point out that willpower alone may not be enough to give up smoking. In the case of smokers their subconscious mind creates emotions that guide them towards smoking and they get a sense of satisfaction from continuing. This is what leads to a mental battle that can undermine our Emotional Fitness, as we shall explore very shortly.

If we allow our subconscious emotional brain to dictate how we think in this way, we can soon find ourselves drinking, eating or using alternative pleasure sources simply to satisfy our short term emotional needs. This is what leads to addictive cycles of behaviour that can destroy us. Ask anyone who has leaned on alcohol, drugs or sex to cope with downward spirals. The emotional part of our brain has wonderful qualities but it can also be a highly destructive force that can rob us of our ability to choose and turn us into its victims. To control it we need to learn to recognise and understand the message behind our emotions and learn to relax when they overwhelm us so that we can chose how we think and feel rather than having choice dictated to us.

Now, let's take a look now at the part of our brain that controls our thinking - our rational brain.

The rational brain

We have discussed how the emotional part of our brain feels our needs. We also have to be able to interpret those needs and decide how best to satisfy them. This is where the rational part of our brain comes in. Situated at the front, the rational part of our brain is our 'thinking' brain. It helps us to identify meaning, review options, resolve problems and make decisions. It has built in creative and logical ability, is the centre of human curiosity and uses the language of 'thought' rather than 'feelings'.

Our internal self talk, the 'voice we hear in our head', is our brain's way of connecting us to our thoughts as we evaluate what is going on around us and weigh up all of our options. Our rational brain receives signals from our senses and from the emotional part of our brain, interprets them and helps us think about how to satisfy our needs. Together the emotional and rational parts of our brain combine to create what I call the brain's FIT process:

F eel (our senses pick up signals - light, sound, taste, smell, touch)
I nterpret (we identify and emotionally interpret those signals (towards - away)
T hink (we make decisions)

It is worth noting here that, before interpreting incoming signals, our rational brain has to identify them by cross-referencing them against what we already know, using our memory[5]. Our memory acts like a giant library, housing all of our life experiences, including all the emotions we associate with past events. If we receive signals that we do not understand, or if we receive signals that remind us of negative past events, we may become alarmed or fearful. This is why many people fear the unknown. This is made worse by the fact

---

[5] Memory is thought to be stored in the organ known as the hippocampus, although the theory of cellular memory suggests that memory may be stored much more widely in all of our cells.

that our long term memory, due to the size of the files, is stored at the subconscious level, the same level at which our emotional brain operates, meaning that our subconscious mind can link past and present events without our rational mind knowing why. This can leave people thrashing around for rational explanations to physical feelings and emotions they do not consciously understand. Let me give you an example.

Sarah approached me because she was afraid of flying. She had experienced a particularly turbulent flight in recent years and, following that flight, was unable to even think about flying without being sick. When Sarah reflected on her past she recalled another flight she had experienced as a seven year-old child when the plane she was on experienced severe turbulence. When the turbulence started she heard an adult behind her say, "The plane is going to crash and we are all going to die" which made Sarah panic. Understandably Sarah was terrified at the time. The memory of this event, stored deep within her subconscious mind, combined with her more recent experience, created an extreme level of anxiety that was disproportionate. Once Sarah became aware of this 'double whammy' she was able to rationalise her problem. By accepting her physical feelings, without letting them dictate what she could do, she was able to choose to regain control. Two weeks later she flew happily away on holiday and even coped well on the return journey, despite flying through a thunderstorm.

This is why therapists often encourage their clients to review past experiences so that they can clarify the link between current and past events and change how those experiences affect the way they feel and think today. Once consciously aware of the link, clients often find it easier to deal with the feelings and emotions they are experiencing.

But whilst understanding the links between the past and the present can be helpful, there is one fundamental principle of

Emotional Fitness, which is worth stating. No one lives in the past or the future, we all live in the present. Enjoying our 'bit in the middle' is something that can only be evaluated in the present moment. Therefore the present is the place where Emotionally Fit people live. The past can only affect how we behave in the present if we allow it to occupy our thoughts. Putting the past behind us and focusing on the present are therefore key to achieving Emotional Fitness.

The fact that we focus a great deal on our past owes a lot to the way our rational brain develops. The front of our brain, which controls so much of our rational thinking, grows significantly during puberty. Pre-pubic children have rational ability but their emotional brain tends to dominate their judgements, which is why their emotions change so rapidly. As they reach puberty however, the front of their brain grows and they experience increasing rationality as their brain prepares them for the move from childhood to adulthood. This is why teenagers can be moody, difficult to relate to and conflict-driven.

This is relevant because it explains why adults sometimes look back on their childhood with critical and often harsh rational judgements about past events. The adult uses their newfound rationality to judge their childhood, which is unfair because at the time their actions would have been driven by a child's brain, rather than an adult's. Unfortunately, this does not stop people from beating themselves up or blaming themselves for things they did or did not do in the past.

The rational part of our brain is a wonderful tool that helps us to analyse and work out solutions to problems. But, just as we should not accept our emotions at face value, so too must we be careful not to assume that our thoughts will always guide us in the right direction. Our rational brain operates largely at the conscious, rather than the subconscious, level. As such, it is excellent at analysing and thinking about what we are experiencing. It can use its creative and logical skills to think about and try to make sense of the past and present and its creativity even allows us to imagine the future and invent things in our mind.

But, as we discussed earlier, our rational brain does not always fully understand our emotional needs, especially our psychological needs, nor indeed emotional reactions born out of subconscious memories. As a result it can resort to over analysing everything in a desperate attempt to find rational answers where none exist. I call this 'irrational rationality' as we find ourselves inventing answers to suit our circumstances and protect ourselves. This in turn sends confusing and often conflicting messages back to our subconscious mind, which responds in the way it responds to all conflict, with emotions of anxiety or fear. This creates a vicious circle in which the rational and emotional parts of our brain pull in opposite directions causing either emotional overwhelm (where our feelings run out of control), or rational overwhelm (where we cannot stop thinking and analysing).

As this causes so many of today's Emotional Fitness problems, let's take a 'time out' here to understand this battle in a little more detail. Understanding this battle won't stop it, but it will help you to recognise it when it happens and in the next chapter we will explore how you can control it.

The emotional - rational battle

To understand why this emotional - rational battle exists we need to understand the function of a small organ in our brain called the **amygdala**. The amygdala sits between the emotional and rational centres of our brain. When the emotional part of our brain senses that we have a need it sends chemicals[6] to stimulate our rational brain, as we discussed earlier. That chemical is also received by the amygdala, the function of which is to sense danger or threat. Tests on animals have shown that when you surgically remove their amygdala, they no longer react with rage or fear in situations that previously resulted in such reactions.

The amygdala is effectively our 'fear' gatekeeper and is important for three reasons. First, it lights up if it senses danger or threat. When this happens it starts a chain reaction triggering our fight or flight response, pumping adrenaline, noradrenalin and cortisol into our body to increase our heart rate and blood pressure, contract our muscles and suppress non-essential bodily functions, like digestion. The purpose of this activity is to transfer blood from non-essential areas of the body to the muscles walls so that we can fight or run away.

If you have ever suffered from stress, anxiety or panic attacks you will be familiar with the physical feelings this generates which can include a racing heart, churning stomach, tingly head, vomiting, loose bowels, tightness in the chest, muscle tension, or a sensation of pressure in the chest. One of the main reasons why people suffer stomach and bowel problems during prolonged periods of stress or anxiety is that the stomach is the largest area of blood supply in the body. When the fight or flight response kicks in, blood is pumped out of the stomach to prevent energy being wasted on digestion which is why people speak of a tightness or knot at the top of their stomach.

---

[6] The emotional part of the brain sends dopamine to the amygdala and the rational part of the brain when we have needs. If the amygdala lights up during this process the organ known as the hypothalamus is stimulated which triggers the fight or flight response. This causes adrenaline, noradrenalin and cortisol to be pumped into our body to excite and strengthen our system.

Constant repetition of this activity caused by continuous stress is what leads to internal physical damage, such as irritable bowel syndrome, ulcers and other stomach and digestive disorders. It can also damage our immune system by starving our immune cells of the blood they need to stay healthy. So, the next time you start to experience anxiety or negative thoughts, pay attention to the correlation between your thinking and that sense of tension at the top of your stomach. Manage that and you begin to master stress.

Recognising and accepting these physical symptoms is important so that you understand (rather than fear) them when they occur naturally during downward spirals. The key is to relax and stop the fight or flight process the moment you sense it. In the next chapter you will find workouts designed to help you achieve this.

The second reason why the amygdala is important is that recent research suggests that its activation stimulates the right pre frontal lobe of our brain, leading to defensive and protective thinking patterns (see diagram 4).

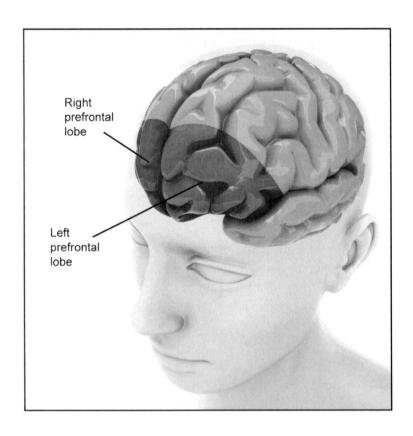

Right
prefrontal
lobe

Left
prefrontal
lobe

Diagram 4

The right and left prefrontal lobes

Research also suggests that if the amygdala does not light up, activity is more prevalent in the left prefrontal lobe of the brain, resulting in more open and positive thinking. Research carried out on Buddhist monks for example has shown them to have much higher levels of left prefrontal lobe activity than other groups, due to the lasting effects of years of meditation. Tests have also shown that people with higher levels of activity in the left prefrontal lobe of their brain appear to recover much more quickly from emotional distress than people with higher levels of activity in their right prefrontal lobe.

This is important because it may even explain why, when we experience downward spirals, we find positive thinking and rational choice so difficult. In downward spirals our emotional needs may have no rational solution. This may trigger our fear response, creating negative, frantic thinking. In order to think positively again we need to calm our system down, restore the amygdala to a resting (or neutral) position and access the left prefrontal lobe of our brain to allow ourselves the opportunity to restore choice. Later in this book you will find a process I call RADAR, designed to help you achieve this transformation.

The third and final reason why the amygdala is important is that it acts as a sort of emotional thermostat, controlling our emotional sensitivity. The important thing to note is that not everyone's amygdala reacts with the same intensity. Some people have an amygdala that is more predisposed to emotional arousal than others. Some people, for example, are naturally shy and anxious, whereas others are bold and fearless. Some people are naturally rational and calm, whereas others are more emotional and reactive. These are crucial differences that affect human relationships.

To emphasise this point a BBC television documentary in 2008 featured a young couple who were always arguing. The wife regularly responded to problems by getting angry, irritable, tense and frustrated, whereas her husband always remained calm and rational, which frustrated his wife even more. To better understand why this conflict was occurring the couple participated in an experiment that involved taking problem-solving tests whilst lying in a brain scanner. When the test results came back they showed extensive amygdala activity in the woman's brain and far less amygdala activity in the man's brain.[7]

Empathy, the ability to recognise and respond to the emotions of others (something we shall discuss in Part 2), is a common trait in most animals, especially humans. However, the extent to which empathy affects our own emotions appears to be influenced by how active our amygdala is. The fact is that different people have different levels of amygdala sensitivity. People with naturally high levels of amygdala activity tend to react to most things from an emotional perspective, often sensing fear when under pressure or threat. They can be more prone to feeling fearful, anxious, worried, or stressed, feel very sensitive to criticism or challenge, see risks rather than opportunities or react aggressively when challenged. People with lower levels of amygdala activity tend to feel calmer, see things from a more rational, analytical, logical, almost "black and white" perspective and may feel slightly uncomfortable with, or detached from, other people's feelings and emotional sensitivities.

Of course, we cannot reach into our brain and fine tune our amygdala, but we can recognise and better understand our natural sensitivities in this regard and consider the impact we have on other people. High amygdala people, for example, may benefit from turning down their reactivity to events, to prevent

---

[7] This is not a male female issue. The results could so easily have been the other way around.

them being prone to uncontrollable emotional outbursts which lead to them being perceived by others as aggressive, needy or 'high maintenance'. Low amygdala people, on the other hand, may benefit from turning up their listening skills and showing more personal interest in people, rather than just focusing on logic and reason, to prevent them from being perceived by others as uncaring, inconsiderate, disinterested, rude, direct and cold.

To identify whether your natural responsiveness is emotionally or rationally biased, why not complete the emotional / rational questionnaire which follows.

Emotional - Rational questionnaire

To test whether your reactions are emotionally or rationally biased simply complete this short questionnaire. Read each statement and then rate it using this scoring system.

Disagree strongly   1 point
Disagree slighlty   2 points
Neutral   3 points
Agree slighlty   4 points
Agree strongly   5 points

Then add up all of your points and enter your total score at the bottom.

		Score
1	I feel I am a rather shy person	
2	I often get nervous before meeting people I don't know	
3	I often get angry with myself or other people	
4	I find it hard to switch off and relax	
5	I react impatiently if I have to wait for things	
6	Small things often irritate me	
7	I get "wound up" when I see people breaking rules	
8	I tend to worry about things a lot	
9	I often feel anxious	
10	I feel like crying during sad films	
11	I often get over excited about things	
12	I often feel depressed	
13	I tend to act a little "over the top" when I'm excited	
14	I often react first and think later	
15	Other people's emotions have a big impact on me	
16	I get easily hurt when criticised	
17	I often feel frustrated	
18	I get irritable when things don't go my way	
19	My moods can be erratic and unpredictable	
20	The thought of failure frightens me	
	Total Score	

Interpreting your emotional / rational score

Score : 20 - 39 high rational responsiveness

It is likely that you see most things from a rational, even black and white perspective. You do not overreact to situations and like to make careful and considered judgements. Some people may see this as cold or calculating. You may appear aloof or cold to others despite your real intentions and you may find it difficult to understand why other people get so emotional.

Score : 40 - 59 mixed emotional / rational responsiveness

Your reaction to events is likely to be unpredictable and varied. Sometimes you may be calm and rational and at other times emotional and reactive. You may not always feel in control of your emotional responses. Others may describe you as unpredictable and perhaps moody.

Score : 60 + high emotional responsiveness

You react to most things emotionally. You may get easily excited in both a positive or negative way. When people or events annoy you, you find it difficult to control your emotions and may get angry or moody on a regular basis. Life is a series of highs and lows and you may find it hard to put things in perspective, especially when things go wrong.

What to do next

If you scored 20 - 39: Spend more time trying to understand other people's concerns or worries. Ask people how they feel and listen attentively when they explain. If you don't understand people's emotional reactions ask them to explain why they feel the way they do and ask them how they think you can help them.

If you scored 40 - 59: You probably have a fairly balanced level of emotional responsiveness, sometimes rational and sometimes emotional. Start to become more aware of the specific situations that automatically drive a higher emotional response from you. Try in these situations to listen more and understand other people's emotions before reacting.

If you scored 60 +: You probably react to most situations from an emotional perspective. Start to recognise what situations trigger physical feelings of increased tension or anxiety in you. When you experience these feelings breathe deeply. Use the RADAR technique you will find later in this chapter (Workout 1 in chapter 1.4) to control your thoughts and feelings if you feel emotionally out of control. If you react consistently the same way use the CLEAR technique (Workout 2 in chapter 1.4).

DART thinking

I suggested earlier that if our amygdala senses danger it not only triggers our fight or flight response but also negative or defensive thinking driven by the right pre frontal lobe of our brain. Having seen so many of my clients develop this type of thinking I have come to describe it as DART thinking:

Defend   Attack   Run away   Tolerate

By learning to recognise and stop DART thinking we can dramatically improve our Emotional Fitness very quickly. Here are some of the most common DART thinking patterns I find people adopt as a result of amygdala attacks.

Defend:

- Creating a **false self image** (joker, mimic etc) to protect themselves
- **Lying** about the issues they face
- **Justifying** their position or wrong actions
- **Distorting** events (over reacting or under reacting)
- **Deflecting** - changing the subject or avoiding intimacy

Attack:

- **Blaming** others for something they feel threatened by
- **Accusing** others of causing their problems
- Expressing **entitlement** to things and demanding attention
- Acting in a **self righteous manner**
- **Lashing out** verbally or physically

Run away:

- **Avoiding** issues or people they feel threatened by
- **Denying** that problems exists
- **Ignoring** warning signs and pretending they don't exist
- **Diverting** attention onto other issues to avoid dealing with problems
- **Self-harming** - seeking comfort in pain

Tolerate:

- **Assuming they are unworthy** of a positive outcome
- **Believing they are defective** in some way
- **Blaming** themselves
- **Constantly criticising** themselves
- **Accepting they are a victim** deserving of punishment
- **Self doubt and self pity**

These are just some examples of the sort of DART thinking patterns our brain can adopt automatically when we cannot satisfy our emotional needs. Such thinking creates *'irrational rationality'*. Whilst we do not have time in this book to consider each of these problems in turn, suffice it to say that, from an Emotional Fitness perspective, learning to recognise these thought patterns helps you by alerting you to the fact that you might have become the victim of an amygdala attack.

In the next chapter we will explore what you can do in those situations to prevent such an attack destroying your Emotional Fitness and how you can choose to change the way you think.

Why not complete the questionnaire which follows, designed to help people identify any DART thinking habits they may have developed.

DART self talk questionnaire

To test whether you have developed DART self talk habits simply complete this short questionnaire. Read each statement and then rate it using this scoring system.

1 = Never
2 = Very occasionally
3 = Sometimes
4 = Quite often
5 = Quite a lot
6 = All the time

	DEFEND	Score
1	If I do something wrong my first instinct is to deny it	
2	I often justify my actions / make excuses when challenged even though I know I may be wrong	
3	If I'm caught doing something I shouldn't be doing my first instinct is to lie	
4	I can be very stubborn when challenged	
5	I sometimes ignore what I don't want to face up to	
6	I often resist help or advice	
7	I often tell myself that I am right even when I know I am wrong	
8	I often refuse to listen to anything I don't want to hear	
9	I ignore criticism or negative feedback	
10	I can be very self-righteous	

	ATTACK	Score
1	I often blame other people when things go wrong	
2	I can be very critical of other people	
3	I can be very dismissive of other people	
4	I hold grudges if people hurt me	
5	I often lose my temper with other people	
6	I find it easier to find what's wrong with things than what's right	
7	I can be very cynical	
8	I often demand that I get my own way	
9	I attack people verbally when I'm challenged	
10	I can be very cutting and sarcastic with people	

	RUN AWAY	Score
1	I often play the joker to hide my real feelings	
2	I say I don't care about things when I really do	
3	I don't let people get close to me for fear of them hurting me	
4	I tend to hide my feelings	
5	I often pretend something is not happening if I can't deal with it	
6	I keep myself busy to avoid dealing with my problems	
7	I often turn to (drink / drugs / sex) to escape my problems	
8	I refuse to talk about my problems and pretend nothing is wrong	
9	I often put off dealing with difficult matters	
10	I often feel I just want to be on my own	

	TOLERATE	Score
1	I often blame myself for things going wrong	
2	I often put myself down	
3	I often think I'm worthless or inadequate	
4	I regularly doubt myself and my ability	
5	I often think of myself as a victim.	
6	I tend to go along with or put up with things rather than stand up for what I really believe in	
7	I often feel guilty or ashamed	
8	I don't expect good things to happen to me	
9	I often think I don't like myself	
10	I often think there is something wrong with me	

What to do next

1. Identify those statements where you have scored 4 or more.
2. Develop a plan to change your self talk and stop doing what those statements highlight

A question of balance

You might think, with all this talk of battles between the rational and emotional parts of our brain, that the most Emotionally Fit outcome would always be the imposition of rational thinking, just like Mr Spock in Star Trek. In reality though, a purely rational approach to everything can actually be detrimental to our well-being.

Take the case of Mr Ellis, a patient of neurologist Antonio Damasio.

Following surgery to remove a tumour, Mr Ellis suffered damage to the area of the brain responsible for integrating his rational and emotional responses. This rendered him incapable of feeling emotions. Because Ellis's emotional and rational responses were disconnected, he was unable to make the most basic of decisions. Faced with a choice of which restaurant to eat in, he would study the menus and restaurant layouts, yet be unable to decide. When shown violent pictures or pictures of naked women, he showed no emotional reaction whatsoever. Ellis had no emotional capability and, as a result, no way of making a decision. Without emotional input Ellis's ability to choose was effectively destroyed.

To function effectively as human beings we need the rational and emotional parts of our brain to work together. Take eating in a restaurant. Just like Ellis, we interpret the words on the menu and conjure up pictures in our mind of what the food looks like (rational brain) but, unlike Ellis, we also imagine the taste and how it might feel to eat it (emotional brain). Now, take shopping. Our brain balances affordability (rational brain) with desire (emotional brain). Think about the last time you argued with yourself about buying something. Your rational brain would have weighed up all the pros and cons but your emotional brain would have been weighing up how owning that item would make you feel.

Achieving balance though, does not mean aiming for perfect harmony. The tightrope walker for example does not achieve balance by remaining perfectly straight. They move from side to side adjusting their balance to one side or another as they go. Life is the same. Sometimes we want our emotional brain to dominate this relationship. We want to experience passion and joy; to get angry in the face of injustice; to feel sad if we lose someone or something precious; to scare ourselves occasionally by stepping out of our comfort zone. We also need to express our emotions outwardly sometimes, rather than keeping them bottled up, because emotions represent energy which, if not discharged, can cause internal damage through retained tension and stress. Letting go emotionally is a key part of being human and we should not force ourselves to be rational and controlled all the time.

At other times though, we want our rational brain to dominate. When we buy a home, negotiate an important deal at work or sort out our financial affairs, we need to lead with a rational approach. Television programmes like **Homes from Hell** show what happens when buyers purchase a property because they fall in love with it (emotion) and then fail to do their homework or check out the developer (rational), resulting in them being conned out of their life savings.

The emotional rational battle lies at the heart of our search for happiness. In an ideal world this battle would always have our best interests at heart, but we don't live in an ideal world. Sometimes, our emotional brain reacts to life's events by highlighting psychological needs which our rational brain cannot quickly resolve. This can lead to anxiety which creates DART thinking and self destructive behaviour designed with only one thing in mind - gaining short term satisfaction. At other times our rational mind reacts to life's events by locking us into negative DART thinking which destroys optimism and promotes "away" rather than "towards" emotions. Searching for happiness therefore relies on us winning the emotional rational battle by recognising it and fighting to restore choice over how we think and feel.

Key learning points

In this chapter we have looked at the science of choice. Here's a quick reminder of the key points to remain mindful of as you continue your journey into the world of Emotional Fitness.

1. All human behaviour is driven by ancient instincts, which use our senses to identify and satisfy our physical and psychological needs.
2. The most common instincts are the **SEARCH** instincts: **Survival - Engagement - Achievement - Reward - Control – Harmony.**
3. The emotional part of our brain "feels" our needs through physical feelings and emotions which guide us **towards** and **away** from things to satisfy our needs.
4. The **emotional** part of our brain possesses self-awareness. This allows us to understand our own mortality and evaluate our **"sense of self"**.
5. The **rational** part of our brain identifies and interprets incoming signals, cross references them with memory and helps us make decisions, using thoughts.
6. We cannot function effectively without emotional and rational input. The aim of Emotional Fitness though, is not perfect harmony. It **is CHOICE.**
7. To achieve Emotional Fitness we need to see our physical feelings and emotions as **messengers**, but not allow them to dictate who we are or how we choose to think and feel.
8. Our emotional needs require **short-term satisfaction.** They can overwhelm our rational brain when solutions are not easily available, especially to our psychological needs.
9. When our rational brain is overwhelmed the amygdala senses fear and triggers our flight or fight response. This in turn triggers the **right prefrontal lobe** of our brain, leading to irrational **DART** thinking strategies: **Defend - Attack - Run Away – Tolerate.**
10. **DART strategies** can convince us that satisfying alternative needs like hunger, thirst or pleasure is a good idea. This can lead to food, drink and other **addictions.**

11. Positive, more rational thinking requires **left prefrontal lobe activity.** To achieve this we need to calm our system down and effectively re-boot our brain.

12. People have different levels of **amygdala responsiveness,** making them predisposed to either rational or emotional responses. Both have advantages and disadvantages and this may affect the level of empathy they show to others.

13. Our brain processes information so fast that **emotions and thoughts often occur before we consciously choose** them.

14. Emotional Fitness is about recognising the emotional - rational battle that can flair up in our mind. It is about **restoring our ability to choose,** before we become victims of our emotional Puppet Master.

In the next chapter we will review the problems that can arise from the emotional - rational battle and examine ways of dealing with them.

Chapter 1.4: Winning the emotional - rational battle

Before moving on to explore in more detail the SEARCH instincts and the emotions they drive, I would like to take a few moments here to share with you some of the simple techniques I have used with my clients to help them cope more effectively with the emotional and rational battle we have just discussed.

The first point I would like to make is that feeling emotionally or rationally overwhelmed is quite normal and common. Such experiences can catch us by surprise though, and take us over if we are not vigilant and prepared. To help my clients cope I recommend different techniques for emotional and rational overwhelm and these are summarised below.

1.4.1: Emotional overwhelm

The most common emotional problems which overwhelm people are:

- Panic or anxiety attacks
- Depression
- Suppressed emotions

So let's briefly consider each of these in turn.

Panic or anxiety attacks.

Panic and anxiety attacks normally occur when people experience some form of stress. On my seminars however I often stimulate debate by suggesting that there is no such thing as stress. This prompts an immediate reaction from some people who take offence and explain how stressful their life is and how pressurised they feel. Of course I understand this totally but what I go on to explain is that one of the dangers today is that we label things and as a result we hang on to those labels and the limiting beliefs which accompany them.

Anne's case of claustrophobia, which I described in Chapter 1.2, serves as a warning that we must be careful not to label our problems in ways that lock us into the belief that we are victims of something outside of our control. To achieve Emotional Fitness we need to take ownership of and deal with the actual symptoms we experience.

Stress, like claustrophobia, is a label. It is a word we use to describe a certain way of feeling. But stress does not exist. What does exist are the physical feelings we experience during an 'amygdala attack'. When our amygdala senses fear it triggers our fight or flight response causing the rapid physiological changes we discussed earlier, which include a churning stomach, increased muscle tension, increased heart rate, sweats and so on. It is these physical sensations that define panic or anxiety, and people often fear these physical feelings more than the actual events which cause them because of the upheaval they create. I have worked with many people for example who, having experienced a sudden emotional shock or panic attack, became obsessed with the idea of those feelings returning, locking their rational mind into a cycle of negative anticipation. The key question is, "Why do so many people experience stress, anxiety or panic?"

In my experience people who describe themselves in this way are normally feeling trapped in some way and whenever people feel trapped, their brain senses a threat to their physical or psychological survival, triggering their fight or flight response. The more this happens the more their brain becomes sensitive to it, looking for it around every corner, which creates a vicious circle. So why do we feel trapped? Feeling trapped is directly related to the SEARCH instincts I mentioned earlier. Because our instincts constantly monitor our needs, we feel trapped whenever our needs are not satisfied. As a result we experience feeling trapped in different ways. For example:

Survival instinct

We can feel trapped when we find ourselves in a confined physical space we cannot escape from, when we are physically in danger or when we are trapped in a negative sense of self.

Engagement instinct

We can feel trapped in a relationship or group or when isolated from the same.

Achievement

We can feel trapped in a job or career, or when we sense a lack of opportunity.

Reward

We can feel trapped in a negative pleasure driven habit, such as substance abuse.

Control

We can feel trapped when control is taken out of our hands or when we feel insecure.

Harmony

We can feel trapped when we are physically ill or mentally locked into past regrets or future negative prediction.

Understanding the causes of our stress, anxiety or panic can help us by allowing us to think rationally about why we feel trapped and make better decisions regarding what to do about it. In the next chapter we will focus on this in more detail, but for now, let's concentrate on dealing with the physical sensations of stress, anxiety or panic. Dealing with the underlying causes cannot take place until we first stabilise the physical sensations, which dominate how we feel and think.

Dealing with stress, anxiety or panic is a two-stage process.

As a young boy, I remember that the early cars did not have synchromesh gearboxes, so changing gear required 'double declutching', a process which involved putting a car into neutral between gear changes. Going from first to second gear, therefore, required a first gear - neutral - second gear sequence. Handling emotions related to stress involves the same process. On the one hand we feel anxious and want to feel more positive immediately but, as we saw from the science in the last chapter, jumping from anxious to positive in one move can crash your gear system because you are effectively trying to jump from right front brain to left front brain instantaneously. Moving into neutral first, disengaging the power, and then changing into the next gear is the best way forward. To achieve this smooth transition I encourage my clients to adopt the **RADAR** method. **RADAR** stands for:

R ecognise (your physical feelings and emotions)
A ccept them
D on't ANALyse them
A pply neutral gear (stop thinking)
R elax and restore choice

This process has helped my clients overcome stress, anxiety and panic attacks and retake control of their lives. The secret lies in **NOT** fighting the physical feelings but accepting them. This does not mean surrendering to them though. RADAR allows you to fight back, but not by trying to work things out rationally whilst you are experiencing the tremors of an emotional earthquake. By relaxing and refusing to allow your thoughts to link to your emotions, creating a toxic partnership, you create a much stronger platform from which you can restore choice when the storm subsides.

This sounds easy, but it isn't. When your body is shaking and your thinking is negative you will instinctively try to fight your way out by analysing your feelings, emotions, and thoughts which makes your tension and anxiety worse. The thing to remember is that feelings of anxiety and panic cannot harm you.

Let me repeat that.

Feelings of stress, anxiety and panic cannot harm you.

Sure they can be very disturbing and uncomfortable, but they cannot, in themselves, harm you. What can harm you however, is allowing your rational mind to become overwhelmed by emotions to the point where you make bad choices and become their victim.

When difficult emotions trigger our fight or flight response we need to declare war on the physical feelings we experience rather than declare war on ourselves, or those around us. RADAR helps people to achieve this by encouraging them to jump from panic to neutral rather than from panic to positive. Neutral is a place where people can pause and recover before choosing what to do next.

At the end of this chapter you will find a full guide to using the RADAR technique (Workout 1).

Sometimes however, panic or anxiety attacks can be stubbornly resistant and in these cases there may be a subconscious link driving them. In such cases, some event in the present triggers our subconscious long-term memory and we suddenly end up re-living past feelings and emotions. These 'echoes' of the past are simply that and should be seen as such but they can be overwhelming if we allow them to dominate our present thinking. To deal with such events I recommend to my clients that they re-programme their mind using what I call the CLEAR technique.

CLEAR stands for:

C hoose
L ocate
E xpress
A ffirm
R eprogramme

This technique involves repetitive re-programming of the subconscious mind to release any past associations and memories, which are automatically stimulating a sense of anxiety or panic. It is simple and easy to do but requires a commitment to following the guidelines and frequency recommended.

Another way of overcoming past 'echoes' is to remind ourselves of the potential we had as a child and restore the confidence and vitality we were born with that sometimes gets lost over the years. Meditating can help this.

At the end of this chapter you will find a full guide to using the CLEAR technique (Workout 2) and a meditation designed to help you put the past behind you (Workout 3).

Depression.

Depression is another big word we use to describe emotional overwhelm. Whereas stress, more often than not emanates from being trapped in situations we do not want to be in, causing a sense of anxiety, depression often occurs without warning causing a much deeper and darker sense of despair. Clinical depression can result from chemical imbalance in the brain or brain malfunction but often the causes of depression are unclear and may result from the non-satisfaction of psychological needs. Anyone suffering from regular or prolonged bouts of depression should always seek medical advice but we must careful not to use the depression label to describe how we feel every time we find life tough. Sometimes we just feel lonely, sad or lost and need to deal with the underlying root causes of those problems rather than labelling ourselves with an external condition over which we have no control.

My own experience of depression taught me that, whilst some may say that depression is a case of mind over matter, it is not as simple as that. Depression can attack suddenly and without warning. When it does, it creates a sensation that I can only describe from personal experience as heavy, dark and oppressive. Winston Churchill called it the 'Black Dog'. When it strikes, the world seems a darker place and the route out seems beyond our capability. In such cases DART thinking dominates our every second and our self-reflection becomes negative. Ironically I found that it also made me resistant to help and made me more self-centred.

Here's my story.

Some years ago I suffered from periods of what I came to believe was depression. I avoided seeking medical support but became familiar with Churchill's 'Black Dog'. I remember going to bed one night feeling fine, only to wake up the following morning with feelings of dread, a sense of despair and the sensation of pressure in my chest and stomach. These feelings sometimes lasted a week, sometimes a few days.

When I first experienced these feelings I began thinking very negatively. I wanted to be alone. I locked myself away in my room and, quite frankly, looking back on it, felt sorry for myself, even though my life was fine. I tried to analyse my feelings but that made me worse. I discovered that when the negative part of my brain was fired up it became better than TV detective Colombo at finding more depressing ways of looking at life. I began thinking in frustrating circles:

"Why am I depressed?"; "I hate my life."

"Why do I hate my life ?"; "I don't know."

"Why can nobody understand how I feel?"; "Because nobody cares."

"Life's not fair"; "I know I hate it."

If anyone offered me help, I became aggressive and short with them, proclaiming: "Go away. You can't help me."

Sounds ridiculous now, but I was actually becoming possessive of my own pain. If someone made me laugh or distracted me, I would momentarily forget how bad I was feeling, but the second I remembered, I was straight down that rabbit hole guarding my depression with my life.

Of course, I now realise that I had allowed negative emotions to hook up with old memories and create DART thinking strategies. I now know what to do about this, but at the time I did not. The problem was made worse by the fact that I convinced myself that leaving my isolation would involve a Herculean effort on my part and necessitate me having to explain to everybody what was going on when I did not understand it myself. I came to the point where I actually got comfort from hiding away because it meant I didn't have to face everyone, and that created a vicious circle.

So how did I recover?

One day I suddenly asked myself two important questions:

"Is the way I feel actually going to kill me?"

and

"Who am I talking to?"

My answers were:

"NO - my feelings are emotionally painful but they won't kill me."

"I'm talking to myself."

I realised in that moment that locking myself away and analysing everything was useless. I began to see analysis as 'ANAL'ysis and realised that, whilst the physical and emotional feelings of depression could overwhelm me at any time for reasons which I might or might not understand, they were not life threatening. Nor were they a true representation of who I felt I was.
    I therefore made two choices.

First, I chose to accept the brutal reality of how I was feeling but decided not to let those feelings stop me doing the everyday things I would have done if I wasn't feeling depressed. If you like, I treated my feelings the same way I would treat cold or flu symptoms, and just got on with my ordinary day to day activities. Did the feelings disappear? Of course not. But I decided to carry them with me and ignore them rather than let them dictate my thoughts. At times this was draining but I stuck at it.

Second, I stopped analysing my feelings, looking for answers and talking to myself about how I felt. I stopped trying to be a false optimist. I just got on with my life without trying to predict when I would feel better, or how.

After a while I noticed that by not analysing my feelings they gradually subsided. Was this an easy road? No. It took willpower, but I decided that this was a battle and that I was going to win it (maybe that was really my first choice). In short, I took ownership of my physical feelings, emotions and thoughts.

Today I rarely experience those feelings, but when they do reoccur, and they do, often out of the blue and probably no more than three or four times a year, I simply say "Oh I've got depression again" in the same way that I might greet a cold and refuse to analyse it or think about it. My teenage daughters have taught me that wonderfully annoying phrase, 'whatever', and although I don't like it when they say it to me, I have found that my emotions find it equally as irritating when I say it to them, so they don't hang around. In forcing myself to do something, anything except ANALyse how I feel, I have found a positive coping strategy that has freed me from the prison of my negative emotions.

By recognising the message behind my emotions (that I needed to put the past behind me and move on in my life) but not letting that dictate my thoughts, I was able to keep choosing positive, rational action. Sometimes, in downward spirals, we have to take ownership of this emotional rational battle and win it. Sometimes we have to find the courage to be honest, face our brutal reality and not allow our emotions to drive us towards destructive thoughts, based on an instinctive desire to satisfy our needs.

I am not suggesting that what I did will work for everyone and I re-iterate the need for anyone struggling with depression to seek professional help, but I also encourage anyone who may be suffering from depression to try the techniques recommended in this book.

At the end of this chapter you will find 10 tips for dealing with depression (Workout 4).

Suppressed emotions

One of the other problems people often face is that they do not feel comfortable expressing their emotions. As a result they often allow their frustrations and feelings to boil up inside and when they eventually do express them they are often expressed in a negative or wholly inappropriate and uncontrollable way. Talking about our feelings however is not always easy, especially to others, and men in particular often struggle to overcome the old mantra of "big boys don't cry". I therefore encourage people to talk openly about their emotions to people they trust and to become more comfortable expressing their emotions. Where emotions are causing hurt or anxiety I encourage people to express these emotions privately so that they can release the inner-tensions, which accompany them.

At the end of this chapter you will find a guide to help you express suppressed emotions (Workout 5).

Now let's consider something which gets discussed far less than it should - rational overwhelm.

1.4.2. Rational overwhelm

Emotional overload is not the only problem people experience when the rational and emotional parts of the brain do battle. People also experience rational overwhelm, the most common problems being:

1. **Inability to make decisions.**
2. **Inability to stop thinking.**

Let's explore these in a little more detail.

Inability to make decisions

Sometimes the emotional - rational battle may not totally overwhelm us but it can interfere with our decision-making ability. Take the example we alluded to earlier of shopping. How many times have you found yourself unable to make a buying decision as you weigh up the emotional and rational perspectives? Or how many times have you faced an important decision and just been unable to make up your mind, something which probably frustrated you?

For such occasions I recommend what I call the RSVP method:

> **R** ecognise the conflict
> **S** top the debate
> **V** erify your concerns
> **P** ostpone the decision

When people experience indecision part of the problem is that they put themselves under immense pressure to decide, which makes their confusion worse. It's a bit like trying to find your lost car keys. You never can when you're panicking, but once you relax their location springs into your mind. Decision-making is the same and the RSVP method helps you achieve this.

At the end of this chapter you will find a full guide to using the RSVP technique (Workout 6).

Inability to stop thinking

Many people simply think too much. Some of my clients had such active minds that they spent nearly all of their time thinking about and ANALysing everything. This condition does not get nearly as much press as emotional problems like panic or anxiety attacks, but rational overwhelm can be equally disturbing and just as debilitating. It can also be extremely tiring, as the brain rarely rests. The problem here is that many of us are simply not used to switching our rational minds off. We become so used to thinking that we don't know how to control it and the rational mind's methodology of reviewing all sides of an argument leads to an internal debate which tortures us. The secret to overcoming this is to recognise that thinking is within our control. We have the ability to start thinking and to stop it.

Stopping thinking sounds easy, but for a highly active mind it isn't because most people have never tried to stop thinking. They often say they have, but what they mean is that they try occasionally for a minute or so and then give up. The problem with thinking is that it happens so fast we are always playing catching up, as we discussed earlier. So we need to first accept that thoughts will occur whether we want them to or not. The secret lies in what we do with them when they do occur. In a moment I will share with you two simple techniques I recommend to help people stop thinking.

First though, please allow me to explain something. When people find themselves thinking too much they often try to relax by closing their eyes. This works for some, but the problem is that loss of one of our most important senses, sight, can cause the brain to think even more as it tries work out what is going on. To test this try sitting down and closing your eyes when you are, say, in a shopping mall. Your mind will automatically start thinking about what is going on, trying to recreate the image of the mall in your mind and starting to bother you with thoughts like: "Are people staring at me?"; "Is anyone coming near me?"; and so on. Whereas closing your eyes can be good for relaxation, the fact is that closing your eyes can actually stimulate thoughts. I therefore recommend that practicing not thinking is best done with your eyes open. This may seem a little strange at first but with regular practice you will begin to master the ability to shut off your thinking with your eyes open or closed.

At the end of this chapter you will find two different approaches to stopping thinking (Workouts 7 & 8).

Key learning points

In this chapter we have considered very practical techniques that you can use to reduce the impact of emotional and rational overwhelm. Here's a quick reminder of the key points.

1. When you experience emotional overwhelm:
    a. Use the **RADAR** technique to deal with stress, anxiety or panic attacks.
    b. Use the **CLEAR** technique if you experience persistent attacks.
    c. Use the top 10 tips for dealing with depression.
    d. Take time out to express your emotions, rather than bottling them up.
2. When you experience rational overwhelm and can't stop thinking:
    a. Practice the **RSVP** technique when you are struggling with decisions. This allows you to postpone your decision making until you are much clearer in regard to the outcomes you want.
    b. Practice the **"stop thinking"** exercises included in the following workouts.

In the next chapter we will consider the SEARCH instincts in an attempt to better understand the message behind our emotions. Before we do however, I have provided next a series of workouts designed to help people cope with their emotional - rational battle. If you prefer, you may choose to move straight to Part 2 and return to these workouts at a later time.

Workouts to deal with emotional overwhelm

Workout 1: RADAR (for stress / anxiety / panic attacks)

R ecognise (your physical feelings and emotions)
A ccept them
D on't ANALyse them
A pply neutral gear (stop thinking)
R elax and restore choice

Recognise

Emotions, as we now know, involve physical feelings and an inner sense of being guided towards or away from things to satisfy our short term needs. When you find yourself feeling emotionally overwhelmed in a downward spiral, focus on recognising the physical feelings you are experiencing and **notice what the feeling is compelling you to move towards or away from.**

Accept

This step is simple but essential. Most people when emotionally overwhelmed immediately try to fight the feeling, which can lead to stress, anxiety and panic attacks. Take comfort in the fact that your brain is creating these sensations to protect you, whilst it may not feel that way, this is their purpose. Accept that the feelings are real but they cannot harm you unless you start to think and behave out of control. This does not mean bottling up your feelings however. If you feel like expressing your feelings feel free to do so, but do not fight or resist them.

Don't analyse

Again this step is crucial. Your rational mind will, once it becomes aware of your emotional problem, want to analyse why it is happening. Such analysis is futile as the reason why you are feeling that way may be far from obvious and may, as we discussed earlier, have more to do with past experiences than present ones. By refusing to analyse how you feel you immediately prevent your rational and emotional brain linking together into a destructive flywheel of negativity based on anxiety. This is not the time to sort out the root causes of any stress.

Apply neutral gear

This may sound the same as "Don't analyse" but it isn't. Once you feel overwhelmed your thoughts may avoid analysis but start to flounder on something else. Focus on your breathing and try to clear your mind of all thought. Many people find this difficult because they have never tried to stop thinking. There are many ways of doing this and you must find one that suits you. I often encourage my clients to imagine their mind as a blackboard and to imagine that blackboard being wiped clean as thoughts appear on it. Some people prefer to imagine themselves far away in a pleasant place to achieve the same effect. Whatever route you choose do NOT dwell on any thoughts that occur to you. Let them come and go.

Relax and restore choice

The secret when emotionally overwhelmed is to breathe slowly, as panic and deep breathing are incompatible. I recommend breathing as follows:

Breathe in through your nose (mouth if your nose is blocked) counting slowly from 1 up to 5; then breathe out through your mouth very slowly, again counting from 5 down to 1. Repeat this until you feel yourself calming down.

This is simple and allows the out breath to fully escape the lungs before taking fresh air in. Panic often involves taking air in too quickly before the stale air has a chance to escape.

Only when you feel calm and relaxed should you then choose how to think and respond.

This process will restore your system to neutral, allowing your brain to access thinking from the front left side of your brain instead of the front right, as we discussed earlier.

Workout 2: CLEAR (for persistent panic / anxiety attacks)

C hoose
L ocate
E xpress
A ffirm
R eprogramme

Choose

Choose a persistent negative emotion you are experiencing and name it, e.g. worry, anxiety, panic, fear, dread, anger, jealousy, etc.

Locate

Try to recall the earliest incident in your life where you recall being disturbed by this emotion (don't try to force it). Do not dwell on or analyse any past events you remember just note them. *If your persistent emotion relates only to a recent event or series of events, with no link to past events, then you do not need to do this, simply focus on the recent events without dwelling on them or analysing them.*

Express

Now read the following out loud to yourself 3 times.

"I want to thank my subconscious mind for protecting me with this feeling of (insert your problem emotion) but I now want all mental pictures, memories, unhealthy beliefs, feelings and any physical ailments related to this emotion to be removed so that I live a happy, healthy life, free from (insert problem emotion). I expect the benefit of this exercise to increase ten times every time I practice."

Affirm

Choose and commit to memory a very short affirmation which reinforces your ability to overcome this emotion (see below for examples). Make your affirmation positive and in the present tense eg "Freeing myself from all .... (insert your troublesome emotion). Remember that your subconscious mind works in the present and will focus on the words you use.

Re-programme

Take a deep inward breath counting *slowly* from 1 up to 5. Breathe out *slowly* counting down from 5 to 1.

Repeat this cycle until you settle into a deep breathing rhythm that suits you.

Close your eyes.

Slowly repeat your affirmation to yourself and after each affirmation imagine seeing yourself in the future how you want to be (focus on what you WILL **look & feel** like, not what you WON'T).

Repeat this continuously for a minimum of 5 minutes.

Open your eyes.

Repeat this cycle a minimum of 3 times per day for approximately 5 minutes each time.

Possible affirmations (or choose one of your own)

Freeing myself from all .... (anxiety / worry / stress/ etc).

I feel positive and energised.

I am calm and relaxed.

I feel powerful and strong.

My body is healing.

Workout 3: Meditation for overcoming the past

Sometimes people struggle to put the past behind them. I find that this meditation helps people who are struggling to leave their past behind. If you are troubled by flashbacks from your past you may find this of benefit. Feel free to adapt it to your particular preferences.

How to use this meditation

Read the text in italics two or three times until you have a clear mental picture of the story. Then find a comfortable place to relax where you will be undisturbed. Sit or lie down and close your eyes. Take a deep inward breath counting slowly from 1 to 5 and then breathe out slowly counting from 5 down to 1. Try to breathe in through your nose and out through your mouth. Focus on your breathing for a few moments and allow thoughts to wander in and straight out of your mind. When you are ready, simply close your eyes and imagine the scene described below. Open your eyes when you are finished.

Note: It may help to play a CD of relaxation or wave music during this meditation or you may chose to complete it in silence dependent upon your personal preference.

Imagine that you are walking along a beach. Take a few moments to feel the sun on your face, the wind in your hair and the texture of the sand beneath your feet. Listen to the sound of the ocean waves crashing on the shore. When you feel fully in touch with this scene, feeling as though you are actually there, I want you to imagine that you see a small figure in the distance approaching you.

As the figure gets nearer, you notice that it is a child. As the child gets nearer you notice that this child is YOU - you from an earlier time in your life. You notice that the child is carrying heavy bags. When you look closer you notice that these bags are full of all the events which have troubled you in your past. Notice how tired the child looks.

Now imagine drawing a line in the sand and ask that young child to put down those heavy bags. Thank the child for carrying those bags for you for so many years. Now invite the child to step over the line and leave those bags behind. As the child steps over the line take them into your arms, give them a big hug and then imagine drawing that child inside your own body. As you do this feel the warmth and energy of that child filling your body and enjoy the sense of excitement and possibility that the child possesses.

Now imagine taking that child on a journey to the future. Show the child all that you can achieve together and promise to keep that child safe and free from heavy bags in the future. Take time to relax during this journey and only when it is complete, slowly open your eyes.

When you have finished write down anything that comes into your mind and continue to add to that list over the course of the next week as things occur to you. This will help you to put the past away and identify what it is that you really want from your life.

Workout 4: 10 tips for handling depression

1. **Stop thinking.** Analysing your feelings will get you nowhere. Use the stop thinking techniques in the next section to help you stop analysing.

2. **Start relaxing.** Practice the deep breathing included in the RADAR technique we discussed earlier for at least 10 minutes three times a day.

3. **Carry your feelings and emotions** like a heavy burden someone has asked you to carry for a short while. Imagine putting them in a rucksack and carry them with you without analysing what's in the rucksack.

4. **Carry on doing your normal daily activities.** Do not give up and surrender to the feeling.

5. Do not turn to alcohol for relief. Avoid it until you are free from depressive thoughts.

6. **Do not isolate yourself.** You may feel like locking yourself away from everyone but don't.

7. Do something to **distract yourself** that will occupy your mind. Clear the loft, clean the car, get absorbed in a hobby. Anything that will focus your mind away from yourself.

8. **Get regular exercise.** Try playing or participating in a sport or simply exercise for around 20 - 30 minutes a day. If you do exercise make it reasonably challenging, even a light jog. Gentle walks may work but can lead to more melancholy if you allow your mind to analyse how you feel.

9. **Do something that's fun.** Watch a funny film, for example, or read a funny book.

10. **Change your environment.** If you do the same thing, the same way and in the same place every day then any change will be difficult. Change your daily habits and do not sit in the same place all the time or occupy the same room doing the same thing.

- **Remember - always consult a doctor if depression is causing you concern.**

Workout 5: Guide to expressing suppressed emotions

1. Do not involve alcohol as it clouds your judgement.
2. Find a quiet place where you will not be disturbed by anyone.
3. Remove all distractions or potential distractions - like the phone ringing.
4. It may help to put on background music to suit your reflective mood (this is a matter of personal preference).
5. Take a deep breath counting from 1 up to 5. Then breathe out counting from 5 down to 1. Then close your eyes and keep focussed on your breathing.
6. Don't try to think about or analyse your feelings just listen to your body and let any emotions rise up.
7. Try to go to the heart of your feelings and emotions. Push into them rather than running away from them or stopping them.
8. Let any tears or expression come naturally.
9. Welcome those feelings as a sign of release - do not judge them or yourself.
10. Try to stay with those feelings as long as possible.
11. When your feelings subside thank your subconscious mind for allowing you to release those emotions.
12. Open your eyes and reflect on your experience as a positive release of unwanted emotion.
13. Write down your thoughts after this session.

Repeat this exercise whenever you feel necessary.

Workouts for dealing with rational overwhelm

Workout 6: RSVP (overcoming indecisiveness)

Recognise

Recognise when you are debating something in your head and are unable to reconcile conflicting ideas.

Stop the debate

Simply STOP debating the problem in your head. Do NOT keep running over the pros and cons in your head. Simply say to yourself, "STOP" or use my daughters' phrase "WHATEVER" and stop the debate.

Verify your concerns

Identify all the negative thoughts you are having. Do NOT try to resolve them. Do NOT restart the debate. Simply recognise what the negative concerns are. For example, you might be thinking "I'm worried I can't afford it", "I don't know if I can do this", "My partner / boss won't like this" and so on.

Postpone the decision

A simple enough idea but put off making any decision for a minimum of twenty minutes. Force yourself to walk away and come back to the problem when the twenty minutes has elapsed. If you still cannot decide then postpone any decision to the following day. Keep doing this until you reach the point where you become clear about what you want to do. If this clarity does not materialise then stop thinking about the matter all together. Put it behind you and move on.

Workout 7: Stopping thinking (option 1)

Step One

Take some deep breaths. I recommend that you take a deep inward breath whilst counting *slowly* from 1 up to 5 - then breathe out *slowly* counting down from 5 down to 1 - then breathe in again. Repeat this 5 times and then continue deep breathing in a manner that feels comfortable. Make sure that all the air in your lungs has a chance to escape when breathing out.

Step Two

Find an inanimate object to focus your eyes upon whilst keeping them open. Do not focus on fast moving objects or scenes involving people moving around or lots of activity. If you do your mind will get caught up in the action, which will promote thinking. Things like a tree blowing in the wind, a lava lamp, a candle flame, or a fire flame are ideal. You might recall in the past watching such a scene and drifting into a daydream. We are seeking a similar outcome here.

Step Three

Keep your eyes fixed on the object without straining them. Blink as you feel the need to. Do not try to think about the object. As thoughts enter your mind (and they will) just allow them to roll in and out. Do **NOT** dwell on your thoughts or worry whether you are thinking or not. Trying to stop thinking starts it! Just relax and let thoughts come and go for approximately 10 - 15 minutes. At some stage you may suddenly become aware that there was a period of time when you were not fully aware of any thinking. This may be only seconds at first but with continued practice you can increase this "thought free" period to minutes.

Workout 8: Stopping thinking (option 2)

Some people find staring at an object difficult because their mind doesn't easily rest. I therefore recommend, for very active minds, that people practice what I call presence. This involves focusing the mind's activity on noticing minor details of what exists around you rather than abstract thoughts about your past, present or future circumstances. It involves dedication to noticing what 'is' rather than what 'isn't' and it can help to relax a mind focused on negativity. Simply follow the guidelines below.

1. Take time out from your day-to-day schedule at least once a day for no less than 15 minutes.
2. Ideally go outside, but you can also complete this exercise inside.
3. Begin by noticing your breathing. Feel and hear each inward and outward breath as you count slowly from 1 up to 5 and from 5 down to one. Pause slightly at the top and bottom of each breath.
4. Notice the texture of your clothes, jewellery or watch.
5. Look around and notice the detail of what you see. Specifically pay attention to colours and shapes.
6. Tune in to every sound you can hear.
7. Select certain objects and touch them. Flowers, trees, bushes, gates, etc. if you are outside or cushions, upholstery, the texture of tiles, floors, books, vases, etc. if you are inside. Anything that captures your interest.
8. Notice what you can smell.
9. Continue in this focus for about 15 minutes.
10. Close your eyes and spend a minute or two in quiet reflection on what you saw before resuming your daily activity.

Part 2: The Principles and Practice

In this part of the book you will discover :

- The six **SEARCH** instincts that influence our emotions
  - Survival
  - Engagement
  - Achievement
  - Reward
  - Control
  - Harmony

- The six **P** principles that lead to Emotional Fitness
  - Perspective
  - People
  - Purpose
  - Pleasure
  - Power
  - Peace

- Simple workouts designed to help you practice the 6 P's in everyday life

Chapter 2.1: The SEARCH instincts

Why SEARCH?

In Part 1, we examined how Emotional Fitness requires an ability to choose how we think and feel, especially in downward spirals. We explored how that ability to choose involves a partnership between the rational and emotional parts of our brain and how that partnership can become a battle when our instinctive needs are not satisfied. We explored how our instincts alert us to our needs using emotions to guide us towards or away from things in order to satisfy those needs. We saw how unresolved needs can activate our amygdala triggering our fight or flight response and DART thinking which overwhelms our ability to think positively. We also saw how fast this can happen and explored ways to cope with the resulting emotional and rational overload.

But coping on its own is not enough.

Coping with the fallout from the emotional - rational battle is only part of the answer. Once we deal with the immediate effects of emotional and rational overwhelm we need to turn our attention to understanding the message our emotions are trying to communicate so that we can better understand our instinctive needs and make better choices when it comes to satisfying them.

So let's take a closer look at the SEARCH instincts and how they affect us.

I developed the term SEARCH to describe the instincts which most affect our Emotional Fitness because, over the years, I realised that, whilst my clients' circumstances were all different, the root causes of their emotional issues were often very similar. For example, they were often:

- Feeling trapped, threatened or afraid of some aspect of their life or had lost belief or confidence in themselves or their abilities
  = Survival instinct

- Struggling in their relationships, either because they were too reliant upon needing others, were taking advantage of others or were being taking taken advantage of themselves by others and not stopping it
  = Engagement instinct

- Feeling lost or worthless. Some had lost or were changing jobs whilst others had simply lost sight of what they wanted from their life. Others had thrown themselves into work to escape dealing with their problems and some had simply given up
  = Achievement instinct

- Finding comfort in pleasure based activities (like food, drink, drugs or sex) and experiencing difficulty overcoming their reliance on those comforters
  = Reward instinct

- Struggling to get the world to conform to their demands, or the way they wanted things done, resulting in anger, insecurity and stress
  = Control instinct

- Mentally focussed on the past or the future, not appreciating the present and constantly worried or experiencing regret, self pity and even self loathing = **Harmony instinct**

I also noticed that in downward spirals many of my clients would experience a low sense of self, or low self-esteem.

It became clear to me that not satisfying their needs often triggered their survival instinct, causing a diminished sense of self. For example, one of my clients experienced a relationship problem that triggered their engagement instinct and emotions of hurt. Additionally though, that problem triggered their survival instinct, causing them to doubt themselves which led to a severe loss of self-confidence. As with so many of today's Emotional Fitness problems it seems that unresolved needs can lead to negative self reflection, the root cause of low self-esteem.

Clearly our SEARCH instincts do not exist in isolation of each other. Failure to satisfy one need can have a knock on effect on our other needs. What we need therefore is the right balance. In many respects life is like a circus act, where the performer spins plates on sticks. The performer's aim is to keep as many plates spinning at the same time as possible. To achieve this they start one plate spinning, then another and so on. As the act progresses however, they have to keep an eye on all the plates to make sure they do not lose their balance and crash. In life, it is not plates but our six SEARCH instincts that are subconsciously spinning all of the time, constantly monitoring and reacting to our needs.

Unless we learn to balance **all** of our instinctive needs and choose positive, rather than negative, ways to satisfy them, our life, like the plates, will come crashing down. Similarly, if we only focus on one or two of our needs, like our need for harmony and emotions of happiness or our need for achievement and emotions of pride, we will remain unbalanced which will restrict our ability to achieve happiness. The problem with many self-help approaches is that they single out specific needs, like our need to find love or wealth, and try to focus our attention on dealing with them to the exclusion of all else. It is my view however, that the only way to achieve lasting happiness is to take a balanced and positive approach to satisfying all of our instinctive needs.

Only when we feel good about who we are (**Survival instinct**), engage positively in two way relationships (**Engagement instinct**), fulfil our potential (**Achievement instinct**), apply self discipline to our pleasure instincts (**Reward instinct**), learn to let go and demonstrate humility (**Control instinct**) and take time out to enjoy being alive (**Harmony instinct**) can we truly hope to achieve happiness. Emotional fitness is a guide to achieving the right balance.

The 6 Ps of Emotional Fitness

Just as physical fitness involves balancing the needs of different muscle groups, so too Emotional Fitness involves balancing the needs associated with each of our instincts. Just as you can follow a physical fitness programme to exercise each of your muscles, so too you can follow an Emotional Fitness programme designed to balance each of your SEARCH instincts. What I found from working with my clients was that they were able to strengthen their Emotional Fitness and overall happiness, not by focussing on one aspect of their life, but by reviewing six key areas of their life which related directly to their instinctive needs. I refer to these areas as the 6 P's of Emotional Fitness. The 6 P's are :

Perspective

We can only achieve lasting happiness if we first love who we are and the life we are given.

People

We can only achieve lasting happiness if we share our love with others.

Purpose

We can only achieve lasting happiness if we respect and fulfill our talent.

Pleasure

We can only achieve lasting happiness if we control our basic desires.

Power

We can only achieve lasting happiness if we stop trying to control everything and everyone.

Peace.

We can only achieve lasting happiness if we take the time to appreciate being alive.

Adding these 6 P's to the earlier SEARCH model completes the Circle of Emotional Fitness (see diagram 6)

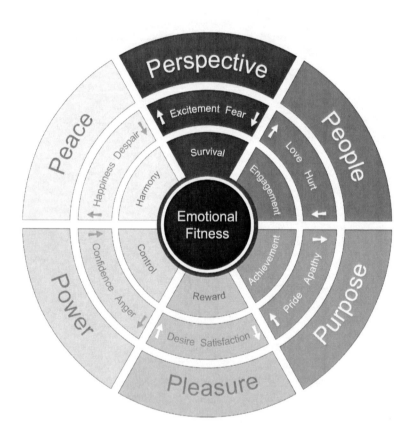

Diagram 6
The Circle of Emotional Fitness

In the next few chapters, we will seek to better understand the message of our emotions by examining each of the SEARCH instincts in turn and exploring :

- Why we have them
- The "towards" and "away" emotions they drive
- How the 6 P principles can help us to positively satisfy our instinctive needs

Finally, at the end of each chapter, you will find workouts and a Stop / Start guide designed to help you find ways of balancing your SEARCH instincts and strengthening your Emotional Fitness. Whether you choose to use these workouts is obviously a matter of personal choice but if you do practice them, you can look forward to the benefits summarised in Table 2.

SEARCH instincts	6 P Workouts	Workout Benefits
Survival	Perspective	A positive sense of self / self-esteem Greater self confidence
Engagement	People	Positive two way relationships Greater sense of love and sharing
Achievement	Purpose	A clear purpose in life Less procrastination - more action Achieving your goals
Reward	Pleasure	Greater self discipline Addiction avoidance
Control	Power	Reduced anger and frustration More positive support of others
Harmony	Peace	Greater appreciation of being alive More fun

Table 2

The benefits of Emotional Fitness Workouts

Chapter 2.2. The Survival instinct

"Courage doesn't always roar. Sometimes courage is the quiet voice at the end of the day saying, 'I will try again tomorrow'."

Mary Anne Radmacher

The first, and arguably the most important, of our instincts is our **Survival Instinct.** It underpins (and occasionally overrides) all of our other instincts and exists for one simple reason: **to keep us alive.** It scans incoming signals from our senses for any sign of threat to our physical or psychological survival. When it picks up such a sign, it uses our amygdala to alert us to danger, as we saw earlier.

In **upward spirals,** we experience the 'towards' emotions of **excitement** (thrill, anticipation, etc.), which help us to interpret threats to our survival as positive. In this way we can enjoy a scary ride or a parachute jump for example. We can step outside of our comfort zone. In **downward spirals** we experience the 'away' emotions of **fear** (panic, anxiety, worry, stress, etc.), which trigger our fight or flight response to alert us to danger. Both emotions serve us but we need to balance the two: too much excitement and we become adrenalin junkies incapable of relaxing; too much fear and we live a life based on self-protection rather than self-fulfilment.

Having a Survival Instinct that protects our physical survival makes perfect sense. As we discussed earlier though, many people don't realise that the emotional part of our brain also protects our psychological survival, reacting to any perceived threat to our sense of self. This is why personal criticism, failure or rejection, can give rise to the same emotions we experience during a physical attack, our brain interpreting such events as a threat to our survival.

To achieve happiness therefore we need to balance our Survival Instinct by managing how we think about ourselves, and the events in our life. In short, we need to maintain a positive **Perspective** and, specifically, develop a positive sense of self. If we do not have a positive belief in our sense of who we are, then our emotional brain will be far more likely to interpret external challenges as a threat rather than an opportunity, thereby triggering our fear response.

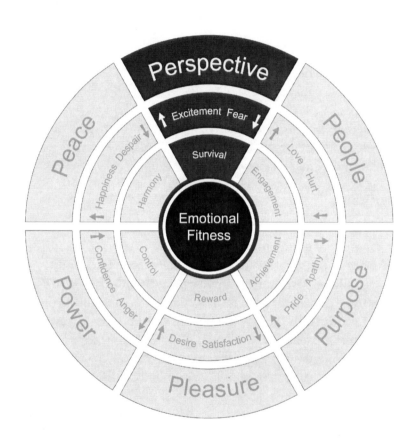

Perspective

Developing a positive sense of self does not mean that we suddenly have to change who we are. That would be impossible. What it does mean is that we have to manage the things which shape our **Perspective**, what I call the four **SELF** principles:

1. S elf-talk
2. E motional control
3. L et go of the past
4. F ind your true sense of self

Managing these four things will ultimately lead to a positive perspective based on a positive sense of self, so let's take a brief look at how these principles work.

Self-talk

The first thing that can make a real difference to our perspective is our **self-talk**. Talking to ourselves is one of the primary means by which we evaluate our world and self-reflect. If we constantly allow the voices in our head to use negative language, focus on negative outcomes and promote negative ideas, the emotional part of our brain will accept the idea that our sense of self is weak and needs protecting. If we keep telling ourselves that we are incapable or inadequate, or that our life is bleak, then pretty soon that outlook defines our sense of self and we become obsessed with self-protection, rather than self-fulfilment. Such an outlook leaves us vulnerable to the constant triggering of our fight or flight response and DART thinking and our emotional brain constantly responds with emotions based on fear, rather than excitement.

I therefore encourage my clients to move towards a more positive perspective, not by re-inventing themselves, but by recognising how they talk to themselves and simply stopping any negative beliefs or thoughts they have. In my experience, when people stop negative self-talk and DART thinking, they quickly begin to feel more positive about themselves and their life. In the absence of constant negative self-reflection they focus on their strengths and opportunities, rather than their limitations and failures. It's amazing how quickly people change their perspective on life by simply refusing to accept negative self-talk. Sounds simple, I know, but it actually takes dedication and practice to stop negative self-talk.

To change your perspective therefore, simply ban negative self-talk. This does not mean that you won't hear it. It is natural for your brain to create self-doubt as part of testing your resolve and evaluating all of your options. What it does mean is that when you hear it you must refuse to accept it, or at the very least do not dwell on it. This applies equally to negative outward talk. Again, this does not mean that you cannot express negative views, but try to avoid general negativity in your speech. For example stop saying how bad things are, how awful the weather is, emphasising problems, predicting negative outcomes, finding faults, criticising, moaning and so on. These are the negative habits that ultimately damage your sense of self. Having a positive perspective is simply about ensuring that you keep your view of yourself, your life and what happens to you in perspective without blowing things out of proportion, negatively or positively.

One thing which can help you challenge your negative DART thinking when you are caught up in a downward spiral is to ask yourself, one simple question, "Who am I talking to?" You will soon realise that the answer is "Myself". Once you realise this, you are more likely to see the futility of negative self-reflection and stop it. Simply saying something to yourself like, "I am better than this " can jolt you back to a place where you stop your negative self-talk. The beauty is that once we stop talking negatively to ourselves and others, positive thoughts pop into our mind. This makes finding our true sense of self much easier because it tends to emerge when the enemy of negativity is silenced. Trying to force a positive sense of self against a tide of DART thinking simply does not work. Create the space and positive things will emerge.

Once my clients have mastered recognising and stopping their DART thinking I encourage them to practice what I call **COPE** thinking:

Can do
Options
Positive questions
Expect positive outcomes

You can adopt **COPE** thinking quite easily by training your brain to:

- focus on what you **Can** do rather than what you can't
- focus on what **Options** you have
- ask **Positive questions,** like "How can I turn this around?", rather than negative questions like, "Why has this happened to me?"
- **Expect** positive outcomes, rather than predicting negative ones.

By disciplining yourself to use these principles for all of your internal self-talk, and external communication, your brain will gradually adopt a more positive way of thinking that reduces your potential for panic, worry or anxiety. This simple but effective change is often underestimated but it can massively boost your sense of self very quickly.

Of course, this won't come easily at first, especially when you are in the grips of a downward spiral, but the fact remains that if you practice controlling your thinking in this way you will be able to do so much more easily in the future.

To develop a positive perspective we can stop negative self talk and outward expression.

Emotional control

The second step in developing a positive perspective is to control how we react to our emotions. In the last chapter we discussed ways to cope with emotional overload and I encourage you to use the techniques detailed there whenever your emotions get out of control. Of course, this can prove difficult when emotions are in full flight, but recognising the signs early and calming your system down before engaging your thoughts is a critical step towards achieving Emotional Fitness. Remember that emotions can't harm you unless you allow them to engage with your thoughts unchallenged. Understanding the instincts in this chapter will help you to better recognise the message behind your emotions and the direction they are driving. The secret is not to allow your emotions to drive you to seek short-term satisfaction in ways, which have nothing to do with the root cause of your emotional problems.

To develop a positive perspective we can listen to our emotions but also challenge them and not allow them to dictate how we think.

Let go of the past

The problem with the past is not that it occurred, but that we allow it to influence the present. As we grow, parents, guardians, siblings, teachers, peers and negative events can have a huge impact on our sense of self, both positive and negative. Think about it. How many times in your life have you tried to copy someone you liked, changed your behaviour because you liked or disliked what you saw someone else do, judged or compared yourself with someone else or done the exact opposite of what someone asked you to do simply to rebel against figures of authority?

And how often do you find yourself recalling past incidents in your life where you failed, felt bad about yourself or lost your confidence? The fact is that our sense of self can become too shaped and defined by early life interactions with others or events. If their influence is positive, this can have a positive impact on our sense of self. If their impact is negative, however, it can lead to us developing a negative sense of self that we carry into adulthood. Some people even develop a false sense of self to protect themselves, as the first success story in Part 3 of this book demonstrates.

Building a strong sense of self requires an ability to put the past behind us. That includes forgiving ourselves and others for past wrong-doing. Carrying guilt or bitterness forward harbours negativity, which damages our sense of self. If other people have done things that are unforgiveable, then we can at least let those things go so that they do not do further damage our sense of self. The simplest thing to do is to agree with yourself right now not to revisit past events in your mind. Distract yourself by thinking about something else whenever you find yourself getting flashbacks to the past. Keep a very positive memory in your mind and think about that memory regularly each day. If negative memories do keep re-occurring then use the RADAR or CLEAR techniques we covered in the last chapter. Remember that YOU can control what you think about. Your mind may, on occasions, flash up "echoes" of past events, especially traumatic ones, but you have the choice not to dwell on the images or thoughts that your mind creates.

To develop a positive perspective we can put the past behind us, not by denying its existence, but by refusing to dwell on it.

Find your true sense of self

Occasionally, changing our perspective requires that we 'look in the mirror' and decide whether we are satisfied with who is looking back. As Carl Rogers, one of the most influential psychologists of the twentieth century, once said:

"The curious paradox is that when I accept myself just as I am…then I can change."

'Looking in the mirror' though, is not easy for two reasons. The first reason is that it requires courage, because it might mean seeing things that we don't want to see or accept. Facing up to who we really are can be a disturbing experience because our emotional brain may interpret such self-reflection as a threat. After all, if you spend thirty years developing a sense of who you are, the idea of changing it, even slightly, can be daunting and so your subconscious mind might resist the change. As a result many people live their lives in fear of who they are, rather than celebrating who they are. Their lives become dominated by DART thinking based on self-protection rather than self-fulfilment.

The second reason is that it means challenging the commonly accepted myth that we have to put ourselves last. On my Emotional Fitness workshops I ask people to list all of the people who are important to them in their life. Less that 20% put themselves on their list and less than 5 % put themselves first. When I challenge this people say, "It's selfish to put myself first". Balancing our Survival Instinct though, is not about putting ourselves first, it is about being comfortable with who we are and what we stand for. After all, when our life reaches its final destination, we will all look back and judge for ourselves whether our life was a true reflection of what we intended.

The Bible says "Love thy neighbour as thyself", it doesn't say, "Love thy neighbour more than thyself". In a plane when accompanying children you are advised to put your own oxygen mask on first in case of emergency so that you can help your children more effectively. Life is the same. We need to strike the right balance between fulfilling our own potential and caring for others but it is a balance, as we shall discuss later when we explore the Engagement Instinct. Everyone has a right, and I would argue a duty, to fulfil their own potential and failure to achieve this can lead to bitterness and resentment.

As someone once wisely said to me:

*"Paul, the rules of life are the same as the rules of golf -
MARK YOUR OWN SCORECARD."*

In this regard, our emotional brain marks our scorecard for us automatically, because it knows what we really care about and what is important to us. As we discussed earlier, our emotional brain monitors our psychological need to feel good about ourselves and we only feel good about ourselves when we live in accordance with the values and virtues we hold dear. If we behave in ways that reflect our values and virtues, then our emotional brain responds with emotions like love, pride, gratitude, empathy and trust. If, on the other hand, we behave in ways that contradict our values and virtues, our emotional brain generates emotions like hate, humiliation, resentment, guilt, distrust, embarrassment, and so on. To prevent these latter emotions dominating our life we need to understand our values and virtues and live according to them. But what exactly are values and virtues?

Values are what we really care about. They are the beliefs we hold to which we have added emotion. For example, we learn many things in our life. Some of those things we choose to believe and others we choose to reject. As a result we end up with thousands of beliefs but most of them are not that important to us. When we add emotion to our beliefs though, they become our values. In other words, beliefs we really care about and seek to defend. Take global warming for example. I believe it is important but, apart from recycling, I am not that emotionally attached to the concept. Someone else however, may be so emotionally attached to it that they join Green Peace. The simple fact is that we all get emotional about different things. Pursuing a life that is aligned with our true values is an important part of maintaining a positive sense of self. If we ignore our values our emotional brain will sense a mis-match between what we really believe in and what we do, causing mental conflict.

What we have to be careful of, however, is that we do not become slaves to our values or adopt negative values. The world is full of examples of people committing atrocities in the name of religious or political values based on grievances. Whilst such activity is values driven, those values are born out of negativity and so promote destructive behaviour. The Dali Lama once suggested that all human beings understand the concept of good and to me this is why, when we pursue values that are destructive towards ourselves and others, we experience mental conflict. Whilst we might be able to justify our actions to ourselves, ultimately that mental conflict destroys us. What we need to ensure is that our values are based on positive outcomes for ourselves and others.

Virtues, on the other hand, are not values. **Virtues are the behaviours or attitudes that we aspire to as a result of our values.** For example, we might value friendship and therefore aspire to virtues of kindness, generosity, thoughtfulness, consideration, reliability, and caring for others. Again our emotional brain understands the virtues we hold dear and if our behaviour runs contrary to our virtues our emotional brain registers the fact, causing mental conflict (something Charles Dickens understood only too well when he invented the character of Scrooge in his book *A Christmas Carol*).

To develop a positive perspective we can define our values and virtues and live according to them without becoming defensive or fanatical.

Perspective workouts

If you want to measure how balanced your Survival Instinct is, why not complete our online Emotional Fitness questionnaire which you will find on our web site **www.emotionalfitnessgym. co.uk** .

In the meantime, to develop a positive PERSPECTIVE and put the principles we have discussed into practice, why not follow the workouts provided below.

For **one week** practice the following every day :

1. Change your self-talk.

Pay attention to your internal self talk. If you start criticising yourself, putting yourself down, blaming yourself, talking like a victim or predicting negative outcomes then shout STOP inside your head. Refuse to dwell on such thoughts and distract yourself either by focussing on something more positive or using the COPE method discussed earlier. Remember that you can change how you talk to yourself.

2. Change your outward talk.

Avoid negative outward talk including moaning, criticising or complaining about things to other people. If you experience problems deal with them yourself calmly, positively and rationally.

3. Control your emotions.

Pay attention to your emotions this week. If you experience emotions which drive you towards behaviour you would rather avoid then use the RADAR technique described in Part 1

4. Let go of the past.

Make an effort this week not to dwell on negative past events. Do not talk about them or allow them to occupy your mind. If you do find yourself thinking or talking negatively about the past just STOP and focus on something more positive.

5. Define your sense of self

- Write down three virtues you would like people to recognise in you (choose from the list below or choose three of your own).
- Focus for one week on behaving each day in accordance with the virtues you have written down.
- Review your progress at the end of each day.

Possible virtues

Care	Joyfulness	Thankfulness
Compassion	Kindness	Trustworthiness
Consideration	Love	Truthful
Courage	Loyalty	Understanding
Courtesy	Moderation	
Fairness	Modesty	
Flexibility	Optimism	
Forgiveness	Patience	
Friendliness	Peacefulness	
Generosity	Perseverance	
Gentleness	Reliability	
Helpfulness	Respect	
Honesty	Responsibility	
Honour	Sacrifice	
Humility	Self discipline	
Integrity	Tact	

Stop / Start guide

Below you will find a few more ideas regarding things you can STOP or START doing in order to develop a more positive PERSPECTIVE on life. I recommend you select one idea from each list and practice them both for 24 hours. Then select another 2 ideas and so on to suit your particular needs.

STOP

1. Believing that you are your thoughts and your feelings.
2. Comparing yourself negatively with other people.
3. Accepting second best.
4. Seeing yourself as a victim.
5. Predicting negative outcomes.

START

1. Asking yourself, "Who am I talking to?" when you start negative self-talk.
2. Using the RADAR technique in Part 1 if you feel emotionally overwhelmed.
3. Focusing on your strengths and what you can do.
4. Believing in yourself and your abilities.
5. Expecting positive outcomes.

Chapter 2.3. The Engagement Instinct

"Love thy neighbor as yourself, but choose your neighborhood."

Louise Beal

The second of our SEARCH instincts is our **Engagement Instinct**, which exists **to encourage social connection and, shall we say, the continuation of the species.** It is one of our most important instincts because our connections with other people have such an influence on what we think and how we feel.

Engagement begins even before we are born. For nine months we are cocooned in our mother's womb totally engaged with and dependent upon her body. Our birth event however, represents a traumatic change, jettisoning us into a state of total disengagement as we enter a new world alone. This event creates in us a powerful sense of separation, and an equally powerful sense of needing to re-engage with our parents, as we cannot survive on our own.

As babies we don't think about our needs though, we just instinctively interpret things like hunger, thirst, cold, or sickness as threats to our survival and cry out for help. Re-engaging provides us with feelings of security and comfort. This is aided by breast milk, which stimulates the release of chemicals[8] in our brain which promote feelings of satisfaction

---

[8] Seratonin is the brain's natural chemical, which calms the body down and promotes the production of oxytocin which promotes feelings of bonding, connection and love.

and calm. Connection between mother and child is also aided by an increase in chemicals during pregnancy, which promote a sense of bonding.

These early experiences of gaining comfort from both personal engagement and the consumption of food and drink is something we carry subconsciously into adulthood. This is why many adults seek comfort in relationships and also food, and drink in downward spirals. The challenge we face as human beings however, is to develop our engagement instinct beyond childhood dependency in a way that allows us to build two way social relationships so that we can breed and connect successfully with others in adult life.

In **upward spirals** we experience the 'towards' emotions of **love** (care, compassion, liking, empathy), which encourage us to connect with others. In **downward spirals** we experience the 'away' emotions of **hurt** (sadness, grief, loneliness), which are intended to motivate us to re-engage. Unfortunately, in downward spirals we often disengage, for example, when we experience bereavement or relationship break up. At these times, we subconsciously remember the pain of separation we experienced at birth and, rather than re-engaging, we avoid contact to escape the pain of separation. Bereavement and relationship breakup can be emotionally difficult because they can trigger a conflict in our mind between wanting to avoid people and at the same time wanting to receive comfort from re-engagement .

Early life experiences of disengagement (like bereavement, being abandoned, being physically or verbally mistreated, being constantly ignored by parents, siblings or peers, or even constantly failing to achieve parental approval) can have a profound impact on our desire to engage with people in later life. Disengagement can damage our sense of self and inhibit our ability to build positive relationships. Many clients I have worked with, for example, have found engaging in later life difficult because of early rejection by their parents or peers.

Clearly, love and hurt carry different messages, but again, we need a balance. We want to love other people, but not to the point where we become dependent on them. We also need to experience hurt, otherwise we would not understand how much relationships matter to us or show concern when we are hurting others, but not to the point where we avoid contact with others to prevent getting hurt. Unfortunately, some people never grow out of their childhood dependency and try to manipulate others for their own personal gain by playing the victim, or appearing incapable or helpless in order to get attention and affection. This may sound cute but it is highly destructive and can make people totally dependent upon others, leading to dependent or exploitative relationships.

Dependent relationships are those where one partner becomes entirely dependent on another for their own sense of self. Again, this sounds sweet, but it can have devastating consequences. If dependent people are lucky and their partner supports them, the relationship can work, but too often such dependency leaves them vulnerable to exploitation. Dependent people are often unable to cope emotionally on their own. They rely too heavily on others and can fail to fulfil their true potential, often blaming others or external forces for their problems. They try too hard to please others in a frantic effort to get love and their sense of self becomes too dependent on people and factors beyond their control. Such relationships become all about manipulation and control rather than genuine love. Recent cases of adults grooming children for criminal purposes is based on them exploiting this dependency in children.

People who suffer from dependency often find it difficult to say "No" to the demands of others. They can become easily manipulated, spending much of their time trying to please other people so that they can get the attention they so desperately crave. My hypnotherapy tutor, Gill Boyne, once told me "Paul, you will never know the meaning of the word *"Yes"* until you fully understand and appreciate the meaning of the word '*No.*' For some of us, saying "No" is difficult. It requires that we stand up for ourselves, resist others' demands, confront people who are trying to force us to do something and reject doing things we don't believe in. Saying "No", however, is the key to avoiding dependency on others. It gives us permission to choose how we feel and think and re-assert our true sense of self.

Exploitation, the other side of the dependency coin, involves using people for the sole purpose of getting what we want. When an exploitative partner stops getting what they want, the relationship turns toxic. They blame the other person for failing them or not meeting their standards. People who enter relationships with exploitation in mind have many reasons. These may include pay back; recompense for hurt they experienced in the past; feeling the need to save someone or even dominating someone in order to restore a sense of personal power.

To balance our Engagement Instinct we can manage our relationships with **People**. Having positive, two way relationships not only helps other people, it also makes us feel good about ourselves. Tests have shown that the emotional centre of our brain lights up more when we carry out acts of generosity than when we help ourselves. This suggests that giving can have a positive impact on our brain chemistry.

People

To improve our engagement with people we can focus on the seven principles behind all successful relationships. I call these the 7 E's which are : :

Expectation
Exchange
Equality
Empathy
Encouragement
Expression
Enjoyment

So let's take a brief look at these principles.

Expectation

Every relationship starts for a reason and brings with it an inevitable sense of **expectation**. Take falling in love for example. At the start it can be fun, exciting and even euphoric as a couple share their hopes, dreams, ideas and plans and enjoy each others' company. Each party is motivated to find out about the new person in their life, showing strong interest in their thoughts and views. Couples actively plan time together, regularly going out and discovering shared interests. Over time, however, the novelty of a relationship can wear off. When that happens people forget why they entered into the relationship in the first place and start to question its value.

This leads to people taking each other for granted and focusing only on what they want out of the relationship and what they are not getting. If not addressed, unfulfilled expectations can lead to relationship breakup, both at home and at work.

To improve our engagement with people we can clarify the expectations of our partners in the relationship and work together to ensure all of our expectations are met.

Exchange

We need to be clear about what we want to get out of our relationships (**the expectation**) but we also need to be clear about what we intend to put in (**the exchange**). Some of us enter relationships focused solely on what we want to get out of them, for example, security, money, status, sex, curing loneliness or feelings of inadequacy. Some of us see relationships as something that will save us, thinking, 'This person will make me feel good about myself'. Some of us see ourselves as rescuers thinking, 'I can help this person and that will make me feel good about myself'. These may seem good reasons. In my experience though, they often lead to toxic relationships when we eventually wake up and think: 'You're not the person I thought you were'; 'You no longer make me feel good' or 'I'm tired of saving you and tired of your problems'. Relationships like these are built on dependency and exploitation. If we allow this to happen we damage our sense of self.

For exchange to be beneficial, it needs to be unconditional. Unconditionality involves giving or loving without looking for something in return. A parent, for example, will normally love their child unconditionally, forgiving and accepting their transgressions and imperfections. Unfortunately, too many people see loving and giving from the perspective of how they feel, rather than how they want their partner to feel. As a result, loving and giving can hide a selfish desire for self-satisfaction. Unconditional loving and giving is not about what we get out of relationships but about what we put into them. Giving conditionally leads to resentment when nothing is received back. Giving without conditions is the only thing that enhances our relationship, and at the same time, our sense of self.

To improve our engagement with people, we can focus on what we put into our relationships, not what we take out. We can give and love unconditionally.

Equality

Equality is a difficult balance to achieve in any relationship. Clearly understanding each other's expectations and what each party is prepared to exchange in a relationship is a start. Often though, a relationship can become a battle of wills based on strength of personality, rather than shared purpose. In such cases the stronger personality can dominate with a negative impact on the other party's sense of self. I have seen many relationships entered into by a partner with a controlling nature and a selfish agenda.

Often a breakdown in equality is caused by a difference of opinion over the roles in the relationship. Who is the main breadwinner? Whose job is more important? How much commitment to a job or career and how much time pursuing it is seen as reasonable? Who wants children and who should look after them? How much free time should each partner have? If the relationship is heavily biased in favour of the needs of only one party, then the relationship quickly becomes unbalanced and deteriorates.

To improve our engagement with people, we can share roles, responsibilities and rewards. We can treat people as equals.

Empathy

As we briefly discussed earlier, we possess a natural sense of empathy, an inbuilt ability to recognise and relate to other people's emotions. Empathy helps us to bond and is the reason why, when we watch other people, we cannot avoid being affected by how they are feeling. It is why we sometimes cry whilst watching a sad movie or wince when we see someone else getting hurt. Empathy is also the reason why we find that ignoring others or shutting them out, a common experience in downward spirals, can cause us to experience mental conflict as we are fight against our natural instinct to connect.

An experiment carried out by scientists on monkeys shows just how powerful empathy is. The monkeys were taught to release a lever in order to receive food, something they mastered very quickly. Later one of the monkeys in the group was wired to electrodes that sent an electric shock to that monkey when the food lever was pulled by the other monkeys. When the monkeys pulled the lever they saw and heard the distress of their fellow monkey and freaked out, leaving the food, even though only one of the monkeys had actually received a shock.

Without empathy we run the risk of our sense of self becoming egotistical and self centred, showing little or no care for those around us. Building successful, lasting and rewarding relationships in our life therefore is dependent upon our ability to strengthen our empathy muscle. Two easy ways to achieve this are:

1. Paying more attention to others
2. Listening to them

To improve our engagement with people, we can demonstrate greater empathy by taking the time to listen more and understand what others are experiencing.

Encouragement

When relationships first start, there is normally mutual interest, time spent getting to know each other, a sharing of thoughts, interests and ideas and a good deal of time spent listening to each other and finding the positives in each other. Over time though, lifes everyday 'stuff' takes over. People become less focussed on the need to put energy into their relationships. When this happens relationships can **CRASH**, resulting in the following behaviours:

C riticism (putting each other down)
Rejection (pushing each other away)
A voidance (avoiding each other)
S tonewalling (refusing to talk)
H olding grudges (refusing to forgive)

Simply by recognising and stopping these trends in your relationships you can dramatically improve them. Three easy ways to achieve this are:

1. Encourage rather than criticise
2. Actively seek opportunities to praise
3. Express your appreciation to others

To improve our engagement with people we can stop CRASH behaviour. We can encourage, praise and appreciate more.

Expression

Having clear expectations, exchange, equality, empathy and encouragement in a relationship are essential, but, if communication breaks down then all is lost. How many times have you seen or experienced situations in which people stop talking and retreat into an internal world of mental frustration? Or worse still, resort to violence as a way to express that frustration? In my work with clients I often find that it is not what people say that causes problems in relationships, it is what they don't say, 'The Unspoken Truth', the real meaning behind what is said.

Take a friend of mine, who once came home after 15 years of marriage to his childhood sweetheart and announced that he was leaving her for another woman. When she asked why, he told her that he had never really loved her. This 'Unspoken Truth' was never aired or discussed. The relationship was doomed from day one.

In another example, one of my clients was brutally treated by her husband whenever he was having an affair. His 'Unspoken Truth' became a reason to punish his wife as she reminded him, every day, of his guilt.

The 'Unspoken Truth' is one of the biggest causes of disengagement and relationship breakdown. Successful relationships are those where grievances, worries, anxieties concerns, complaints, grudges, annoyances and other niggles can be openly aired and discussed positively without judgement or retaliation. Unfortunately, too many relationships do not mature to this level. This is when TRUTH becomes:

The Reality Underneath That Hurts.

To avoid this trap, we need to take a 'time out' in our relationships to review what is working and what isn't and express how we feel. This can be as formal (or informal) and as frequent (or infrequent) as you like but it makes a huge difference. It can renew a relationships by reminding people why they got together in the first place and can help all parties to air hidden "truths". Sitting down with your partner, family member, friends, boss, and even customers or suppliers and reviewing what's working and what isn't is a really healthy process, provided you enter the process prepared to listen rather than defend.

To improve our engagement with people, we can avoid the 'Unspoken Truth', by expressing our thoughts and feelings sensitively and openly.

Enjoyment

Finally, perhaps the simplest principle of all in relationships, and the most forgotten, is the need to have fun. Most relationships start from a positive basis with a desire on both sides to engage. Again, over time the "stuff" of life takes over and we stop going out, stop doing things together and stop having fun. Or we find ways of having fun separate from each other. From time to time we need to restore the effort we put in at the start of our relationship and find ways of doing things together that are fun.

To improve our engagement with people, we can spend time with those we live and work with, for the sole intention of having fun.

People workouts

If you want to measure how balanced your Engagement Instinct is, why not complete our online Emotional Fitness questionnaire which you will find on our web site **www. emotionalfitnessgym.co.uk** .

In the meantime, to develop your PEOPLE engagement skills and put the principles we have discussed into practice, why not follow the workouts provided below.

1. The 7 E's

Use the 7 E's principles to review a personal or work relationship and identify actions you take to improve that relationship.

2. Help others

For **one week**, commit to doing the following 5 things each day.

1. Help people who need it without expecting anything in return.
2. Express your appreciation to, or praise, people who help you.
3. Spend extra time with at least one person you care about at home and at work.
4. Stop speaking negatively and critically about other people or judging them.
5. Look for opportunities to "make someone's day" every day.

3. Stop / Start guide

Below you will find a few more ideas regarding things you can STOP or START doing in order to develop positive relationships with PEOPLE in your life. I recommend you select one idea from each list and practice them both for 24 hours. Then select another 2 ideas and so on to suit your particular needs.

STOP

1. Saying "Yes" when you mean "No".
2. Trying to please other people to get affection.
3. Letting people exploit or control your life.
4. Exploiting people by using them to satisfy your own emotional or physical needs.
5. Avoiding problems in your relationships.

START

1. Spending time alone to reflect on and be comfortable with who you are.
2. Giving your full attention to the people you are with.
3. Giving and loving unconditionally without looking for a payback.
4. Looking for opportunities to be kind / make someone's day.
5. Discussing problems or your feelings openly to avoid the 'Unspoken Truth'.

Chapter 2.4. The Achievement Instinct

"Surely a man has come to himself only when he has found the best that is in him, and has satisfied his heart with the highest achievement he is fit for."

Woodrow Wilson

The third of our **SEARCH** instincts is our **Achievement Instinct**, which exists for one simple reason: **to help us recognise and fulfil our potential.**

I believe that we all understand the idea of making the most of our talents and abilities. When I ask people on my seminars if they consider themselves to be competitive I get a mixed response. But when I ask them to put their hand up if they enjoy losing then, surprise, surprise, no hands get raised. What I believe this demonstrates is that, whilst not all of us are competitive, we all like to feel good about what we achieve.

The Achievement instinct therefore is not about winning or losing. There are many people who have found that winning only destroyed their life and the lives of people around them, ask Tiger Woods. Achievement is about fulfilling our personal potential, which is the only type of achievement that really boosts our sense of self. Competing with others is natural and even helpful in terms of stretching ourselves but in truth, the only real competition we ever face, is against ourselves.

In **upward spirals** we experience the 'towards' emotions of **pride,** which encourage us to do our best and enjoy the experience. In **downward spirals** we experience the 'away' emotions of **apathy** (disinterest, lethargy, procrastination), which try to protect us by minimising the relevance or importance of achieving (which is why people who lose direction often minimise their need to do better). Again we need a balance. Too much pride and we become egotistical and self-centred. Too much apathy and we become so detached that we grow to be disinterested in everything.

To balance our Achievement Instinct therefore, it is vital to establish **Purpose** in our lives, for without purpose we have nothing to focus our potential on.

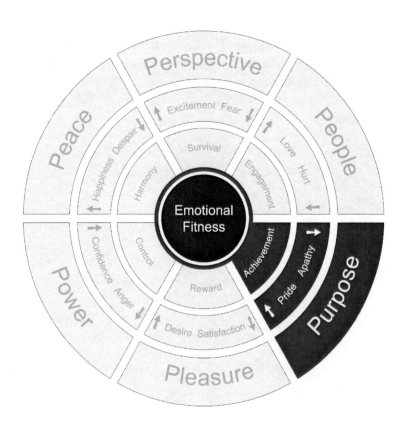

Purpose

Finding our **purpose** means being clear about what we want to achieve. This does not mean however that we have to run for President, build a business empire or achieve a gold medal. It simply means that we have to be clear about and comfortable with the path that we are taking. We can be the best postman, refuse collector, electrician, carpenter, plumber, pop star, comedian, acrobat, tailor, jockey, musician, entrepreneur, artist, sportsman, doctor, nurse, mother, father, son, daughter and so on. What we do is actually far less important than the fact that we do something, which we see as being worthwhile. In my experience it is when people lose direction, or when they know the direction they want but do nothing to pursue it, that they suffer from Emotional Fitness problems. This often misquoted extract from Louis Carroll's *Alice in Wonderland* captures perfectly the risk of not knowing what you want.

"Would you tell me, please, which way I ought to go from here ?"

"That depends a good deal on where you want to get to," *said the Cat.*

"I don't much care where," *said Alice.*

"Then it doesn't matter which way you go," *said the Cat."*

"So long as I get SOMEWHERE," *Alice added as an* *explanation.*

"Oh, you're sure to do that," *said the Cat, "if you only walk* *long enough."*

Some people instinctively know what they want. They have a natural desire to climb mountains, travel the world, tackle the biggest challenges, go somewhere no one else has ever been. Others harbour a strong desire to be a pilot, doctor, nurse, singer, footballer and so on. For some however, purpose emerges by accident, or even arrives out of adversity, as they get passionate about making a change in their own life, or in the lives of people around them. National heroes like Ghandi,

Martin Luther King and Nelson Mandela for example rose to become inspirational leaders because of their determination to fight injustice. Such moments are MOD's (Moments Of Determination). Moments in life when we say 'No' to the way things are. Moments when we shout, **"I am better than this,"** or **"things can be better than this."**

For many however, knowing what they want can prove elusive. Sometimes people are therefore, better off asking themselves what they don't want. This prompts them to identify changes they may want to make in their life. So if you are putting up with something in your life that needs changing then consider making it your purpose to change it.

Another route to finding your purpose is thinking about your strengths.

Every one of us has strengths.

Let me repeat that.

Every one of us has strengths.

The problem is that, often unwittingly, parents and teachers (and in later life, managers) tend to focus more on what we do wrong than what we do right. I read somewhere that by the age of 16 the average child has heard the word 'No' 148,000 times and that the most common phrases we hear every morning before 9 a.m. are 'don't' and 'can't'. To find our strengths we have to look inside ourselves and overcome the bias of others. We have to recognise what we are good at and make the most of that talent. Yes, of course we also have limitations (a word I much prefer to weaknesses) and we need to be mindful of improving where we can. Making the most of our strengths though, is where, psychologically, we can gain the quickest and the most sustainable wins.

A word of warning though. There are two potential pitfalls when it comes to achievement. The first is to avoid letting other people dictate what we can achieve. Many young people, for example, hit downward spirals when their parents break up, when their family life becomes violent and destructive or when their parents become addicted to self-destructive behaviour. This can lead to them seeking comfort from friends who are going through similar problems. The bond of shared pain is a powerful connector but if their friends turn to self-destructive habits, like alcohol and drug abuse, they can easily find themselves drawn into a similar path. Sometimes finding our path involves walking a lonely road. Reliance on others can seem attractive, but it actually inhibits our journey rather than helping it. Achieving our true potential should always be about what we want and not what others manipulate us to want. Sometimes we have to prove ourselves to ourselves and that can involve 'going it alone'. After all, where is the pride in achieving success we have not really earned ourselves.

The second pitfall is not to confuse what we are trying to achieve with who we really are. This point often confuses people, so please allow me to elaborate. Whilst we should certainly celebrate our achievements, if we fall into the trap of defining our sense of self in terms of our possessions, awards or achievements, then we run the risk of losing sight of who we really are. We are not our achievements and achievements alone will never fulfil our sense of self. Similarly, if we try to achieve things by pursuing goals and ambitions that run contrary to our true values and virtues, we run the risk of destructive mental conflict. This is why so many materially successful people, especially celebrities, self-destruct, realising that, despite their success, they do not know, or in some cases, even like, who they are.

Some of the clients I have worked with spent so long pursuing their career or business plans that they lost sight of their sense of self. When their personal career treadmill stopped they found that their life had no firm foundation because pursuing their goals had become who they were. Achieving material success is not a bad thing but, from an Emotional Fitness perspective, pursuing goals that undermine your true sense of self can be counter productive.

Whatever the origin of your purpose in life, whether it stems from a positive dream or adversity, whether it's a determination to change the world, do well at your job or be a good parent, just fix your mind on the outcome you want and take action continuously to get it. Always though, make sure that what you are chasing enhances, rather than damages, your true sense of self.

Once you know the goals you want to achieve, however, you need to take action to achieve them. The problem is that many self help books emphasise the importance of setting goals and making plans, yet I know many people who knew what they wanted, spent hours developing brilliant plans but failed because didn't take action. More important than goals and plans, therefore, is developing an emotionally fit mindset, one committed to action. I therefore encourage my clients to develop what I call a **BOB** mindset. **BOB** stands for:

Brutal reality
Optimism
Bias for action

I began referring to the BOB mindset after being inspired by the story of **Admiral James Bond Stockdale** (December 23, 1923 – July 5, 2005), one of the most highly decorated officers in the history of the United States Navy.

Stockdale led aerial attacks from the carrier Ticonderoga during the 1964 Gulf of Tonkin Incident. On his next deployment, while Commander of Carrier Air Wing 16 aboard the carrier USS Oriskany, he was shot down over enemy territory on September 9, 1965 and was held captive as a prisoner of war in Vietnam for over seven years in what became known as the Hanoi Hilton. Despite being regularly tortured, he refused to give away vital information and even disfigured his own face to prevent him being exploited in propaganda videos. He helped many of his men to survive their physical and psychological ordeal by allowing them to pass on non-essential information when their torture became unbearable. He also taught them a code of secret knocking noises so that they could communicate whilst in solitary confinement.

When interviewed by Jim Collins for inclusion in his book Good to Great, he was asked: "Who didn't make it out?" Stockdale replied, "The optimists." Whilst that may sound strange, Stockdale went on to explain that optimists set unrealistic expectations, focused on external solutions and ultimately suffered from broken hearts. Stockdale put his own Survival down to a simple mindset which has stuck with me ever since and which led me to adopt the BOB philosophy.

He said:

"You must never confuse faith that you will prevail in the end - which you can never afford to lose - with the discipline to confront the most brutal facts of your current reality, whatever they may be."

Admiral Stockdale never lost sight of his end goal. He wanted freedom and was determined to survive to get it. But in order to achieve that goal he developed a mindset committed to dealing with his daily **Brutal reality**, rather than allowing his circumstances to overwhelm him. He maintained **Optimism**, but optimism built on his unswerving belief that he would achieve freedom in the end (without predicting its timing, because that was beyond his control). He fixed his focus on what was in front of him and not on recriminations, blame or things that might happen in the future (again, over which he had no control). Every day he developed a **Bias for action**, doing whatever needed to be done each day in order to survive.

Throughout his time in that prisoner of war camp, Admiral Stockdale never stopped making choices. He chose to face his brutal reality. He chose not to allow his feelings to overwhelm him. He focused on what he could control, rather than what he couldn't. His story is an outstanding example to us all when we face downward spirals that might tempt us into surrender or self-pity. His story goes beyond positive thinking to remind us that the road to achievement requires effort, tough choices, persistence, determination and even pain at times. It means confronting our brutal reality and accepting the pain involved, but not allowing that pain to decide how we think and feel.

Stockdale provided us with a new definition of optimism which we can all use to prevent our mind becoming overwhelmed and discouraged by the question we learned to ask as children when travelling on holidays, "Are we there yet?" Optimism that prejudges the timing and nature of outcomes sets us up to fail by giving us false hope, which is often dashed. Nelson Mandela's passion for the freedom of black people in South Africa contributed to the end of the Apartheid regime. Whilst he achieved his goal however, the path he took, which included 27 years of imprisonment, could never have been predicted at the start of his journey.

Optimism is the belief that we can succeed in the end without worrying about the 'when'.

Sometimes we have to overcome the brutal reality of life, not by ANALysing it (as I call it) or wishing it were different, but by doing what it takes in each moment of each day. Al Pacino expressed this brilliantly in the 1999 film *Any Given Sunday*. In the film Pacino plays a football coach struggling to save his career and overcome a self-destructive lifestyle. In the final stages of the film, in true Hollywood style, he addresses his team before they play the most important match of his and their lives.

This is what he says:

> *"You find out life's this game of inches, so's football.*
> *Because in either game, life or football, the margin for error is so*
> *small.*
> *I mean, one half a step too late or too early and you don't quite*
> *make it.*
> *One half second too slow, too fast, you don't quite catch it.*
> *The inches we need are everywhere around us.*
> *They're in every break of the game. Every minute, every second.*
> *On this team we fight for that inch.*
> *On this team we tear ourselves and everyone else around us to*
> *pieces for that inch.*
> *We claw with our fingernails for that inch.*
> *Because we know that when we add up all those inches,*
> *that's gonna make the ******* difference between winning and*
> *losing,*
> *Between living and dying ...*
> *...That's what living is - the six inches in front of your face."*

Now, you may think, 'These are great stories, but life is not like that.' I disagree. The recovering alcoholic or drug addict, the depression sufferer, the person who's business is failing, the person who loses their job or the person who loses a loved one, all face a tough, inch by inch battle, to fight for better times. And the statistics we saw earlier show that every day more and more people are facing an inch-by-inch battle against emotional and rational overwhelm.

In downward spirals life can be a daily battle for the inches, which, as Pacino reminds us, "Make the difference between winning and losing, between living and dying". The key question we have to ask ourselves is, "Are we prepared to fight for those inches?" In this regard, the biggest enemies we face in fighting for those inches are apathy and it's twin brother procrastination, that creeping mental disease which fills our mind with excuses like:

- 'I can't'
- 'I'm not good enough'
- 'I'll do it later or tomorrow'
- 'It's not that important'
- 'I feel awkward / embarrassed'
- 'I don't know how to...'
- 'I'll get someone else to do it'
- 'I'll get round to it later'
- 'I need to do something first'
- 'I need to get myself sorted out first'

Ring any bells?

These are the **DART** voices of procrastination that destroy our potential and we listen to them at our peril. Make a commitment now to shoot them on sight. If you become their victim you will never achieve. Procrastination is the biggest killer of dreams and goals but action is its kryptonite. Remember that many successful people achieved success not because they had goals, but because their dreams, coupled with their commitment to taking action, led them to be in the right place at the right time, which allowed them to take advantage of opportunities that presented themselves.

Consider this story.

A young man once dreamt of becoming a successful entrepreneur. He wanted to make money so badly he could taste it. He thought about his strengths and decided that he could be an outstanding motivational speaker.

He imagined himself standing in a huge park in front a massive crowd pouring forth his views on how to be successful.

He made a plan and put it into action. He invested time and money booking a venue, inviting people to attend, building a stage, booking support acts to improve the chances of people attending the event. Eventually the day arrived and he fulfilled his dream. One thousand people turned up and everyone left delighted with the show.

That night he sat in the pub working out how much money he had made. He was slightly disappointed to work out that, taking everything into account, he had broken even. He consoled himself however that his effort was worthwhile because it moved him towards his goal.

Whilst he was doing this, a man sat next to him and asked him what he was doing. He explained and when he had finished he asked the man what he did. "I make money," the man said. Intrigued, the would-be entrepreneur asked, "How do you do that?" The man answered "I keep my eyes and ears open and my heart big."

Further intrigued he pushed the man to explain more. "Well take today," said the man, "I was walking past this park when I saw a huge crowd. It was hot so I drove straight to the wholesalers and bought all the ice cream I could get my hands on. I borrowed a cart from a friend and set up in the park selling ice cream. I made two thousand pounds," he said. The young man never forgot the lesson.

The simplest advice I give my clients therefore is this:

"If you want to achieve anything in your life keep your eyes and your ears open and your heart big and keep fighting for those inches, even when every part of you screams, 'Give up'."

As Al Pacino said, the inches we need are all around us but unless we take them when we see them, success will always be harder to find. Are you looking?

The power of visualisation

BOB reminds us that achieving anything is about facing our reality (no matter how brutal), expecting positive outcomes (not predicting the timing), and committing to always taking action. But there is no point facing reality if we don't believe in our ability to succeed in the end. Whilst that sounds simple it often isn't because **you cannot half believe in something**. If you half believe in something half of your rational mind doubts that it will happen and protects you by expecting the worst at some stage. This confuses your emotional brain which does not know whether to move towards or away from things. As a result the energy of your effort is never 100%.

To achieve anything therefore you have to ally the rational and emotional parts of your brain, as we discussed earlier. You have to not only think something is achievable you also have to feel it and to achieve that you need to visualise eventual success, feel the joy that it brings and rehearse it's achievement over and over again. Some have suggested that doing this somehow connects you with Universal energy and perhaps they are right. All I know however, is that doing this puts the rational and emotional parts of your brain on the same page and when that happens your brain is more alert to noticing opportunities that fit with your goals and aspirations and you are more motivated to take them for the simple reason that you don't doubt them when they arrive.

The problem, as Stockdale pointed out, is that too many people visualise success but try to predict when and how it will happen and become disheartened when their predictions prove to be false. Successful visualisation is the imagining of an end result without self doubt and unhampered by exact predictions regarding when and how success will come.

Purpose workouts

If you want to measure how balanced your Achievement Instinct is, why not complete our online Emotional Fitness questionnaire which you will find on our web site **www. emotionalfitnessgym.co.uk** .

In the meantime, to develop PURPOSE in your life and put the principles we have discussed into practice, why not follow the workouts provided below.

1. Use the 10 step method below to achieve one goal.

1. Write down one goal you want to achieve in the next week. This might be something new you want to achieve, something you want to change, something you want to start or something you want to stop doing in your life.
2. Develop a picture in your mind of what achieving this looks like this (draw it if you prefer).
3. Write down how achieving this goal will positively affect you (include how will it make you feel) .
4. Write down five actions you will take to achieve this goal with dates and times.
5. Make a list of negative thoughts you might have that would make you procrastinate and stop you achieving this goal.
6. Now make a list of more optimistic thoughts to stop yourself procrastinating.
7. Write down any barriers or obstacles that might prevent you from achieving your goal.
8. Now write down how you will overcome those barriers.
9. Tell someone about your goal and ask them to check whether you achieve it.
10. Visualise achieving your goal at least three times every day for 5 minutes each time.

Stop / Start guide

Below you will find a few more ideas regarding things you can STOP or START doing in order to develop a sense of PURPOSE in your life. I recommend you select one idea from each list and practice them both for 24 hours. Then select another 2 ideas and so on to suit your particular needs.

STOP

1. Allowing other people or events to dictate your direction.
2. Waiting for opportunities to find you.
3. Focusing on what you CAN'T do.
4. Relying on other people to do things for you.
5. Procrastinating and making excuses.

START

1. Clearing the clutter in your life and prioritising what you want to achieve.
2. Looking for opportunities that might lead you to what you want to achieve.
3. Focusing on and talking about what you CAN do.
4. Setting daily goals, no matter how small.
5. Taking daily action, no matter how small.

Chapter 2. 5. The Reward Instinct

"An unfortunate thing about this world is that the good habits are much easier to give up than the bad ones."

Somerset Maugham

The fourth of our **SEARCH** instincts is our **Reward Instinct,** which exists for one simple reason: **to satisfy our needs.** After all, if we felt no sense of reward from satisfying our needs, we probably wouldn't bother trying.

To understand our reward instinct we first need to understand the concept of conditioning. Conditioning is the process by which our brain learns through repetition.

Since Pavlov first experimented with dogs, getting them to salivate at the sound of a bell on the expectation that the bell would deliver food, we have understood the importance of conditioning in all animal and human behaviour. If we repeat an action often enough we create a pathway in our brain, which makes it easier for us to recognise and repeat the same action in the future. Repetition helps us to learn by storing ideas, concepts and patterns in our memory.

This is assisted by our brain's ability to distinguish between pleasure and pain. Our reward instinct helps us to satisfy our needs by associating pleasure with actions that satisfy our needs and pain with actions that sustain them. **In downward spirals** our needs are not met and so we experience pain and the 'towards' emotions of **desire** motivate us to take action to satisfy them. **In upwards spirals** our needs are met and so we experience pleasure and the 'away' emotions of **satisfaction** guide us away from the object of our desire. Try not eating for a few days and you will soon see what I mean. Your emotional brain will sense your pain and create a desire for food. Once you eat, you experience pleasure and your desire for food will subside leaving you with a feeling of satisfaction that guides you away from food. Again we need the find right balance. Too much desire and we become addicted to pleasure. Too much satisfaction and we become too comfortable, lazy and de-motivated.

The problem with this process, as we discussed earlier, is that our needs are short term in their focus. They demand instant satisfaction and if that is not possible, our desire for satisfaction may overwhelm our thinking. This can result in us trying to find any form of satisfaction, regardless of whether it is related to our original need or not. Negative habits develop because something provides us with a sense of satisfaction, comfort or relief. The pleasure or satisfaction we get motivates us to repeat the activity and through repetition it becomes our automatic response, especially when our psychological needs are not met. This is why people turn to drink, drugs, sex and other pleasure-based habits when they experience downward spirals. Repeated often enough, these temporary solutions become learned habits themselves that we come to rely on whenever we experience unsatisfied needs.

Some of the most common negative habits we experience today start when we experience emotional events in our life. For example, we start smoking or taking drugs, not because they are nice, but because our friends are doing it and we want to fit in; we find comfort from eating in times of crisis; we find comfort in sex at times of anxiety or frustration; we find comfort in inflicting pain on ourselves at difficult times to give us a sense of control over our life and we abuse alcohol to take away anxiety or worry.

Whatever the trigger, once established, we become dependent on these habits for our sense of satisfaction or happiness, relying on them to feel good about who we are. Overcoming such habits is difficult because we are always battling the fact that our brain associates pleasure with the habit we have established and pain with its removal and, as we know, our brain is programmed to avoid pain as part of our Survival Instinct. The secret to balancing our Reward Instinct is to manage our relationship with **Pleasure** so that we enjoy it, without letting it enjoy us.

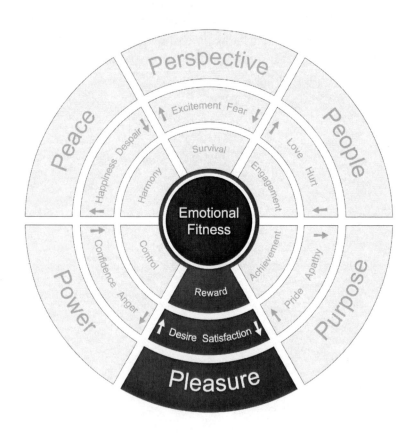

Pleasure

To avoid pleasure becoming the only means by which we seek to satisfy our needs, which leads to addictive habits, we can practice self discipline by focussing on the **IDEAL** principles:

I dentify negative habits
D eclare war
E nvironment
A lternatives
L ive your values

Let's take a brief look at the **IDEAL** principles here.

Identify negative habits

The starting point for balancing our reward instinct and our relationship with pleasure is to identify negative pleasure driven habits that undermine our true sense of self and make us feel bad about ourselves. The problem however is that people often deny the importance or even the existence of addictive negative habits and refuse to get help as a result of DART thinking. When that happens the emotional worry associated with losing the benefits they get from their habit leads to people 'burying their heads in the sand'. Only when they face up to the fact that they have lost control over their ability to choose their own behaviour can they hope to exercise control over their habit. This is why alcoholic support groups insist on people admitting their habit to others. Denial is one of the DART habits that destroys our true sense of self.

Now most of us are not addicts but we may have developed pleasure-based habits that undermine our true potential. Over eating and alcohol consumption are good examples of the sort of modern health habits that become compulsive, rather than chosen. Any time that we find ourselves constantly reproducing the same pleasure behaviour over and over again we need to recognise that we have become the victim of a conditioned habit. Whilst we may say that we can stop it if we choose to, the fact is that people with such habits rarely choose to stop. The smoker, the drinker, the comfort eater, the sex addict, the gambler and other habit addicts all share the same problem: they are not choosing their behaviour, their behaviour is choosing them.

Habits are the result of conditioning and the first step to overcoming them is to acknowledge the brutal reality of their existence.

Declare war (on the right enemy)

Conditioned habits are hard to change, after all we spend many hours practicing them. Our sense of self, though, is always undermined when we allow our feelings, emotions and thoughts to be dictated by our instincts, rather than by conscious choice.

Identifying negative habits and deciding to change them sounds fine, but frankly it's not enough. The power of our unwanted habits is strong and needs more than just a decision to change them. We need to literally **declare war** on the physical feelings and emotions that drive any habits we want to change. This does not mean declaring war on ourselves, or the object of our habit. What do I mean? Take overeating or drinking. Many people declare war on the eating or drinking but that is futile. We have to eat and drink to survive, so our Survival instinct will resist attempts to not eat or drink. When this happens we give up the diet and then feel bad about ourselves. Similarly, the whole concept of not doing something is negative which is not a good starting point for change. Losing weight is about losing and nobody wants to lose.

What we can do however is declare war on the actual physical sensations and emotions driving our habit. By recognising the physical sensation and sense of 'towards' or 'away' that we experience when we feel compelled to carry out our habit, we can use the **RADAR** technique we discussed earlier to pause and reconsider whether we want to carry out that action. By recognising the early signs of bad habits in this way, and refusing to allow them to dictate to us, we stand a much better chance of exercising choice.

No one can force us to do (or not do) what we put our minds to. In many cases though, we have not chosen our habit, we have just allowed conditioning to allow it to choose us. Getting righteously angry about that abuse of your freedom and declaring war on it will help you to create the energy for lasting and committed change. If you recognise the feeling of being compelled to eat but refuse to eat at that moment, choosing to eat later, the motivation later will be different, allowing you greater choice. This allows you to diet not by giving up food but by not being dictated to in terms of when you eat. When you are not feeling compelled to do something you are always in a much better place to choose.

The second phase of declaring war on negative habits is to understand the pleasures our habit is giving us, and how we justify it. All habits, as we have discussed, begin because we associate pleasure with them. Work out therefore, what pleasure you are getting from your habit. Be as specific as you can. For example, does your habit make you feel good about yourself, relax you, excite you, thrill you or simply relieve boredom? Once you understand the pleasure you are getting, ask yourself how you are justifying it to yourself. For example, people often say to themselves:

'It's ok because ...'
   'I deserve a little treat occasionally ...'
   'I'm not harming anyone ...'
   Work out how you justify your pleasure. What is it that you say to yourself that gives you permission to keep performing

your habit? Having done this, re-assess whether you are prepared to declare war on those thoughts. Saying to yourself, "I am better than this habit" will remind you of your potential.

To overcome conditioned habits we can declare war on the emotions, feelings and thoughts that support them, rather than on the habits themselves.

Environment

So, we have declared war, but the next step is to identify what triggers your negative habit. Declaring war on your feelings and emotions that trigger them is only the start because you will also have subconsciously associated your habit with certain times and activities. For example, smokers feel the urge to smoke most when they wake up, visit a pub, meet friends, take a break at work or get in their car. People who overeat often find that they eat when they watch television or when they are bored. People who drink too much, tend to drink in the evenings when they reflect on good and bad days, both being justification for celebrating or drowning their sorrows.

To change persistent negative habits, we have to change the timing of our behaviour and our relationship with the environment that stimulates that behaviour. For example, by not watching television at the same time every day, we can break the link between television and our habit of eating or drinking whilst watching. By keeping busy, we avoid the eating and drinking that comes naturally when we are bored. So, the next step is to work out what activity your negative habit is attached to (e.g. watching television, sitting at you desk, driving home). Then work out what time you perform your habit (when you get to work, first think in the morning, when the kids come home from school, etc). Changing these two things will have a direct impact on the frequency with which you perform your habit, as we shall see in the next steps. Some consideration should also be given to changing your environment. One of the problems with prisoner rehabilitation is that when the offender returns home they often return to the same toxic social environment that encouraged them to commit crime in the first place. If your environment does not change when you want to change your habits, then change will be that much more difficult to achieve.

Whenever changing a habit therefore, I encourage you to find ways to change your environment so that it looks different. Simple things, like: moving the furniture around; going to work using a different route; cleaning your car and putting in a powerful air freshener to change how your car smells; changing the position of your desk or your computer; changing the position of your television or the chair you watch it in, and so on, can help enormously when you are trying to establish new habits. Ensure these changes relate directly to changing how the environment where you perform your habit looks. The impact of changes to your environment, coupled with the other IDEAL measures we are discussing, gives you a far greater chance of breaking your negative habits and restoring your Reward balance.

Overcoming conditioned habits can be easier when we change our environment to remove negative subliminal associations.

Alternatives

Now that you know the triggers, timings, rewards and environment that underpin your negative habit, you come to probably the most important part of changing it, choosing an alternative. As we discussed earlier, we are programmed to seek pleasure and avoid pain, therefore giving up our pleasure habits is potentially painful. So, overcoming negative habits requires a commitment to what we CAN DO rather than what we CAN'T DO.

We need to find alternative habits based on what we CAN DO. Take dieting. The problem from the start is that diets focus on losing weight and in my experience no one likes losing anything. What we need to focus on is what we CAN eat rather than what we CAN'T eat. The problem with many health experts is they recommend that we lose weight by eating food we have never eaten before (and probably never will again outside of our diet), or adopt eating habits that are unnatural to the way we live.

What works far more effectively, if you want to lose weight, is working out what you like eating and then identifying the quantities of it that you can eat and still lose weight. Obviously you need to use common sense when it comes to balancing your diet. Eating chocolate only is not going to make you healthier and will create more cravings for food. But to start losing weight you can achieve quick results by keeping your diet the same and simply reducing the quantities. Trying this for a week can establish a new habit, reduce your resistance to change and from there you can work out how to substitute alternatives into your regime or keep making gradual reductions in the volume of food you eat. In Part 4 you will find a case study that demonstrates how successful this can be. The key point is that whenever you try to change your eating habits it is your self talk and the emotional resistance you experience that will fight you. That battle is made much easier when you substitute alternatives rather than relying on self denial.

I have focused here on weight loss here but the principle is the same for all habits. To remove them we need to find compelling alternatives that will reward us, but which are better for us. Choosing alternatives based on what we CAN DO is the secret to changing all negative habits.

Choosing alternatives does not just include alternative activities, but also alternative self-talk. We saw in the Reward section how people justify their habit in their self talk. It is therefore important to choose alternative self-talk that commits you to your new alternative habit. Often, such self-talk is called affirmation, but at its simplest it is simply saying positive, rather than negative, things in your self-talk. Something like, " I enjoy eating x" or "I enjoy exercising" is all it takes. If you find yourself justifying breaking your new habit and returning to the old habit, then recognise the negative self-talk you are using to justify the change and stop it, immediately replacing it with something more positive.

Overcoming conditioned habits is much easier when find positive, attractive alternatives.

Live your values

Overcoming addictive habits is never easy because, as we discussed before, our subconscious mind associates pleasure with the habit and pain with its removal. The strongest motivation for people to change such habits comes when they see their habit as an enemy rather than a friend. Reminding ourselves of our true sense of self and specifically our values and virtues, we can begin to see our habits as undermining our lives and that can provide the motivation we need. I sometimes ask my clients to imagine that they are describing their habit to an audience of family and friends and ask them to consider how proud they would feel if they had to do this in real life. Exposing their habit in this way can help them find the strength to fight it.

To overcome conditioned habits we can remind ourselves of our own value. We can view negative habits as enemies undermining our true sense of self.

Pleasure workouts

If you want to measure how balanced your Reward Instinct is, why not complete our online Emotional Fitness questionnaire which you will find on our web site **www.emotionalfitnessgym. co.uk** .

In the meantime, to develop a positive relationship with PLEASURE and put the principles we have discussed into practice, why not follow the workouts provided below.

1. Use this 10 STEP technique to overcome unwanted habits

1. Identify a negative pleasure habit you want to give up.
2. Write down what you think triggers this habit (list what you are doing when you start to think about undertaking your habit, e.g. when I am alone, when I go to the pub, when I watch television).
3. Write down the times of the day when you normally perform this habit.
4. Write down alternative things you could do instead of this habit (make a list of things you would enjoy doing but which are better for you than your old habit).
5. Write down how you could change your environment (how could you make the place where you perform this habit look different to remind you of your commitment to change).
6. Write down any negative thoughts or excuses you normally use to support this habit.
7. Now write down more positive thoughts you can adopt to challenge your old habit and support your new habit.
8. Close your eyes and imagine explaining your old habit to an audience of friends and family.
9. Write down : " I will stop this habit on ....(insert date).
10. Visualise performing your new, more positive habit at least 3 times a day for 5 minutes each time.

2. Stop / Start guide

Below you will find a few more ideas regarding things you can STOP or START doing in order to develop a positive relationship with PLEASURE in your life. I recommend you select one idea from each list and practice them both for 24 hours. Then select another 2 ideas and so on to suit your particular needs.

STOP

1. Eating, drinking or adopting other negative habits when you are bored.
2. Accepting you can't change.
3. Setting yourself easy / low standards.
4. Following repetitive routines in everything you do.
5. Making excuses for any negative habitual behaviour.

START

1. Identifying your negative habits and tackling them one by one.
2. Raising your personal standards in all areas of your life.
3. Asking yourself everyday "Is what I'm doing a true reflection of my values ?"
4. Asking yourself each day, "Am I proud of my behaviour".
5. Practicing fasting and abstinence at least one day a week.[9]

---

[9] If you have a medical condition that requires tight food control, such as diabetes, choose something other than food or drink to give up once a week, such as watching TV.

Chapter 2.6. The Control Instinct

"Anger is just a cowardly extension of sadness. It's a lot easier to be angry at someone than it is to tell them you're hurt."

Tom Gates

The fifth of our SEARCH instincts is our **Control Instinct,** which exists for one simple reason: **to protect our security.**

Most of us are familiar with the idea of control. Our early years are dominated by it in one form or another. Direction, advice, guidance, opinions, thoughts, persuasion, cajoling, insistence, and so on from parents, guardians, siblings peers and countless others. From the moment we are old enough to act with independence we are expected to conform to rules and social norms imposed by others and we soon learn to use rules based on our own concept of right and wrong.

Watch any group of children playing and you will soon see arguments about the rules of the game, what constitutes fair and unfair and who is in charge as they copy what they learn from adults. How many times have you seen a child storm away from other children for example shouting "that's not fair"? Control is the means by which adults condition children to abide by rules. Control is the basis upon which organisations and governments impose order and the rule of law within communities. Without individual and group control anarchy would reign supreme.

Our control instinct also exists to protect our security. It creates in us a sense of ownership and competitiveness so that we can defend what is ours. After all, animals mark their territory and fight to protect their food, homes and families and we humans are no different. Animals battle for territory and tribal leadership. So do we. Watch any two year old cuddling their favourite toy when another child snatches it away. Once the initial look of shock leaves their face, the child who has had their toy taken away, more often than not lashes out in the direction of the child who stole it in an attempt to regain possession. All animals understand the concept of 'mine' because possession is a key part of controlling what we need to survive. We instinctively protect what is ours, and that includes our beliefs and values as well as our possessions. This is why some people get so angry when they are challenged.

In **upward spirals** we experience the 'towards' emotions of **confidence** to help us take action. In **downward spirals** we experience the 'away' emotions of **anger** to motivate us to seize back control. Balance here is essential. Too much confidence and we can become too demanding and controlling and too much anger and everything becomes a battle in which we can destroy our relationships by taking out our anger on others every time something goes wrong. In this highly competitive modern world of ours however we cannot afford to respond with anger all the time. We need a flexible approach to control because challenge is inevitable and if we stick too rigidly to a mindset based on making everything and everyone fit our perception of the world, then we run the risk of regular conflict with others.

People with powerful **control** instincts can find it extremely difficult to compromise or let go however. They can be extremely competitive and whilst competition is healthy, obsessive competitiveness can be destructive, ego driven and selfish, driven by a desire to achieve only one outcome - getting their own way. They can become dependent on feelings of power to reinforce their sense of self and this can lead to them trying to impose themselves, their beliefs, values, rules and expectations on others. This is often accompanied by a strong sense of righteousness or intolerance of injustice that fuels their aggression.

Some people with strong control instincts also suffer from obsessive compulsions, experiencing a sense of added security and comfort from repeating minor actions over and over again. I once saw a man suffering from Obsessive Compulsive Disorder (OCD) being interviewed. After spending literally hours rearranging some of his ornaments he was asked why he did it. He explained that it made him feel that his family would be safe. On the face of it this makes no logical sense, but to someone with a highly active control instinct it makes all the sense in the world. After all, if you are worried about the safety of your family, and you know that you can't control it all of the time, it makes sense to focus on something you can control instead, like the position of ornaments ('irrational rationality'). Such obsessive behaviour is exhausting however, and can become all consuming as the person feels compelled to repeat the action over and over again to ensure their feeling of security is maintained.

To balance our Control Instinct therefore, we can manage our relationship with **Power.**

Power

To manage our relationship with Power we can focus on the **REACT** principles which focus on our :

R ules
E xpectations
A nger
C ommunication
T olerance

Let's briefly consider the **REACT** principles.

Rules

Because people build their knowledge, beliefs and values slowly over time, and because they become attached to them, often defining themselves according to them, they can become stubbornly resistant to any idea of change. This results in people creating rules which they impose on their own lives and the lives of others.

Rules, undoubtedly, have a place in civilized society and we all have the right to defend what we believe to be right. The reluctance to question our rules, the inflexibility to change them and the inconsistency and hypocrisy involved in imposing them on others whilst not adhering to them ourselves though, are uniquely human failings. How often do we see judges, politicians, policemen, parents, and teachers preach one set of rules, only to be later caught breaking those rules themselves? How many times do we see motorists protesting angrily when someone cuts them up on the road only to do the same to someone else a few moments later? To achieve Emotional Fitness we need to review our rules and ensure that they reflect our true sense of self and have a positive, rather than controlling, intent.

To balance our relationship with power we can question our rules and our right to impose them on others.

Expectations

Expectations are not rules, they are our view of what other people should and should not do. Parents are legendary promoters of the philosophy that they know what is best for their children. Sometimes they may be right, but there are many times when they are not. To have high expectations for the achievements of others can be a positive thing but, if those expectations become judgemental, then we need to recognise that our expectations of others are more a statement about our own bias and prejudices than a genuine willingness to see others succeed.

Parents have to walk a fine line when it comes to balancing their expectations for their children with their need to allow their children choice in what they do. Whilst every parent should encourage their child to achieve their potential, there is a huge difference between encouragement and controlling force. Many virtuoso musicians or sports stars were encouraged to start at an early age but others were forced to undertake countless hours of practice whether they enjoyed it or not. Achieving the right balance is difficult, but it needs to be a balance and all parents, guardians and teachers should search their soul by asking one question of themselves: "Am I encouraging or enforcing?" If the answer is the latter then I recommend that they restore a better balance by encouraging rather than forcing.

The justification for forcing others to do what we want them to do is often, "It's in their best interests" but that is not always the case. Sometimes our desire to protect those we love, to see them do well, to see them secure, to see them avoid the mistakes we have made in our lives, can lead us to behaviour based on **control** rather than encouragement. One mistake I often see parents making is trying to relive their lives through their children, constantly pushing them or pulling them based on mistakes they made in their own lives, rather than allowing their children to make choices for themselves. I remember once at school at the age of 12 a friend of mine stating:

"When I have kids I'm going to bring them up exactly the opposite way to the way my parents brought me up."

When I enquired, "Why what's wrong with you?" he quickly protested,

"Nothing. I'm fine"

"Then why change it?" I enquired.

He didn't answer and the lesson stuck with me (and I suspect him).

To balance our relationship with power we can avoid the trap of forcing our expectations onto others, born out of self-interest.

Anger

You may have been surprised by the fact that I have included anger as one of the emotions that is triggered by our Control Instinct. The reason is that I differentiate between anger and aggression. Aggression is what arises as a natural self-defensive mechanism when we are attacked and it is fear's natural ally. Anger, however, normally arises when we reach a point where we feel insecure or when we sense that we are losing control in a situation. For this reason anger is often unprovoked and reactive and is, in my view, a response linked more to our Control Instinct and sense of insecurity than our Survival Instinct.

In order to manage anger, which is a volatile and rapid emotion, you can practice the **WATCH** principles:

W alk away
A void
T ime
C ount
H umour

Let me briefly explain how these **WATCH** principles help.

Walk away

No rocket science here. When you find yourself in a situation that starts to get you agitated and frustrated, recognise the early warning signs such as rising tension and simply walk away, even for a few minutes. Only re-enter the situation when those feelings have subsided. By recognising the early warning signs you avoid reaching the point where your frustration explodes into anger.

Avoid

If you think about it, there are certain situations that are more likely to push your anger buttons than others. These differ for each of us but people with a highly active Control Instinct tend to dislike queuing, being told what to do, poor service, waiting, being cut up on the road and so on. By identifying the situations that are most likely to get you angry, you can plan to either avoid them or to behave differently when they occur, because you were expecting them and have prepared how you intend to respond.

Time

Re- visiting your relationship with time will help reduce the potential for outbursts of anger. The reason is that people with a high Control Instinct tend to want things done immediately. This hinders their ability to cope when things go wrong and running late for appointments or meetings is one of the primary causes of their anger. Allowing more time and being more realistic about how long things take, can dramatically reduce anxiety, frustration and the chances of anger outbursts. Some of my clients, for example, plan meetings that run back to back with no break in between and suddenly find the day's events, phone calls and emails catching up with them. By re-organising their diary to build in recovery and planning time they feel less frustrated and angry. Similarly, people when travelling often do not build in delay time. If your journey normally takes one hour then allow an extra $1/2$ hour for the inevitable traffic delays. Better to arrive early than late in a state of panic. This is not a time management book but changing your relationship with time can dramatically reduce your anger levels.

Count

The old adage 'Count to 10' is good advice because it is physically impossible to be angry and relaxed at the same time. If you are running late, therefore, or caught up in a sequence of events that is causing you frustration, take just a couple of minutes to reduce your breathing rate. This simple technique will dramatically impact your mood faster than anything else. Just sit down, even in your car, and breathe in counting from 1 to 5 very slowly. Then breathe out slowly counting from 5 down to 1. Repeat this 10 or twenty times and then go about your business. The RADAR technique included earlier in Part 1 can help here too.

Humour

Seeing the funny side of things is normally something that seems impossible when we are angry but often, when we look back at how we behaved at the time, we find it amusing. Trying to see the funny side of things takes effort but if we can achieve it, anger can dissolve into laughter almost instantaneously. I have lost count of the number of times that people have told me about an incident that got them really enraged and then begun laughing when they think about how it affected them.

Obviously, not all incidents are funny and that is why we shall soon be talking about the importance of communicating our anger in appropriate ways. But when we feel ourselves losing control, it can help to see the funny side. Sometimes imagining how silly you look to others when you get agitated can help. Before you explode next time therefore look around at the people watching you for a few seconds and imagine seeing the expression on their faces if you started to kick off. Another trick is to keep something in mind that makes you laugh. Think about it just as you start to get angry and stay thinking about it until your anger is under control. Personally, I use scenes from television or films that involve people falling over or doing crazy things. That particular archive has helped me to stay calm on a number of occasions.

To balance our relationship with power we can recognise and control our anger.

Communication

Most anger is frustration inappropriately expressed. One way of preventing this is to express your feelings calmly but forcefully. By expressing your feelings, you let people know you are experiencing frustration, anxiety or hurt, in a manner more likely to encourage them to help, rather that fight you. Try something like, " I'm feeling really frustrated and having great difficulty not losing my temper right now and I need your help". This allows you to communicate your anger without threatening the person you are speaking to and by expressing your anger this way you release some of the hidden pressure.

One of my clients was having trouble with their children. Every time he confronted them about their inappropriate behaviour an angry row would break out with no winners. I advised him to do nothing when he saw the inappropriate behaviour but very shortly afterwards to sit the child down and explain that their behaviour had annoyed him and explain why. I suggested he praise the child as being better than their behaviour and expressed how disappointed and let down he felt by their actions. Shortly afterwards, he reported a dramatic improvement in his relationship with his children. Expressing our feelings calmly restores balance - not **power**.

To balance our relationship with power, we can verbally express how we feel, rather than bottle it up until it overflows.

Tolerance

Emotional Fitness requires a commitment to practicing tolerance, something not easy for those with powerful control instincts. Tolerating other people and allowing them the space to live their lives according to their own rules and expectations, rather than ours, can prove difficult. In a world where overcrowding is a living reality this challenge is stretching some people to their limits. Too many people wanting to do the same thing at the same time and in the same place, gives rise to road rage, till rage, service rage and other highly visible outbursts of anger. For the ultra competitive amongst us, this is a huge challenge. Whilst competition is healthy, for some people being competitive is simply a bad habit. Over competitive people are often highly judgemental, critical and intolerant of others, driven by the belief that their view of the world is the right one.

If we try to live our lives by filtering out anything that threatens our sense of self, beliefs or values, we condemn ourselves to a life of defensiveness and conflict, both of which destroy our well-being. We have to be mindful therefore, that our competitiveness does not imprison us in a world limited to 'my way'. If we are to enjoy Emotional Fitness, we need to practice the art of tolerance. This means allowing others to make mistakes and avoid constant judging and criticism of others.

To balance our relationship with power, we can show tolerance by recognising that we have more to learn from others by accepting them, rather than judging them.

Power workouts

If you want to measure how balanced your Control Instinct is, why not complete our online Emotional Fitness questionnaire which you will find on our web site **www.emotionalfitnessgym. co.uk.**

In the meantime, to develop a positive relationship with POWER and put the principles we have discussed into practice, why not follow the workouts provided below.

1. Rules / expectations

- Write down as many examples as you can of rules or expectations that you impose on others at home or at work.
- Review those rules to see if they are fair and reasonable and whether you have informed others why these rules are important to you.

2. Anger

- Write down a recent situation where you got angry.
- Close your eyes and relive that situation again in your mind and consider :
- What triggered your anger (be specific eg the way I was spoken to)
- What were you thinking at the time
- What stopped you controlling your anger
- Identify ways in which you could avoid such situations in the future.
- Identify alternative thoughts you could have to prevent your anger.
- Review how the WATCH principles in this chapter could prevent such anger.
- Visualise yourself in similar situations in the future behaving without getting angry.

- Practice this visualisation at least 3 times every day for 5 minutes and always before entering a situation that has made you angry in the past eg before driving to work, before going shopping, before meeting someone you don't like etc.

3. Stop / Start guide

Below you will find a few more ideas regarding things you can STOP or START doing in order to develop a positive relationship with POWER in your life. I recommend you select one idea from each list and practice them both for 24 hours. Then select another 2 ideas and so on to suit your particular needs.

STOP

1. Imposing your rules or expectations on others.
2. Trying to predict or control every outcome.
3. Worrying about things unnecessarily.
4. Getting angry when things go wrong.
5. Bottling up your feelings.

START

1. Developing positive rules and expectations.
2. Praising rather than criticising others.
3. Practicing the **WATCH** techniques to control anger.
4. Listening more to others and talking less.
5. Learning to let go of what you want and sacrifice or compromise.

Chapter 2.7. The Harmony instinct

*"Every now and then go away, have a little relaxation, for when
you come back to your work your judgment will be surer. Go some
distance away because then the work appears smaller and more of
it can be taken in at a glance and a lack of harmony and
proportion is more readily seen."*

Leonardo da Vinci

The sixth and final SEARCH instinct is our **Harmony Instinct,**
which exists for two simple reasons, **to maintain our sense of
well-being** and **to keep our body in balance.**

Well-being is a concept hardwired into our brain that
includes a natural balancing system called homeostasis.
Homeostasis balances our body through the regulation of vital
bodily functions like temperature, water balance and blood
sugar levels. When we get too hot we sweat to bring our
temperature down. When we are too cold we shiver to create
internal heat and our metabolism slows down to reserve energy
when we experience extremely low temperatures. Our immune
system also works constantly to automatically fight off
infection and protect us from disease.

Our Harmony Instinct is the primary reason why I
suggested earlier that we need to balance our instincts, because
our brain can sense when our body is out of balance and when
that happens our immune system comes under attack. This can
leave us vulnerable to disease. Our immune system works to
protect us but, like everything else, it needs time to recharge its
batteries. When we are calm and relaxed, blood flows to the
cells of our immune system restoring and strengthening them.
When we are stressed, however, our fight or flight reactions

cause blood to flow away from our immune cells leaving them vulnerable to deterioration. If we constantly experience stress and anxiety because our needs are not being met, the constant change in blood flow can damage our immune system, leaving it incapable of fighting off disease when we most need it.

Because the emotional part of our brain protects our psychological as well as our physical needs, our Harmony Instinct is sensitive to any imbalance in our sense of self, in the same way it is sensitive to an imbalance in our physical well-being. In **upward spirals** we experience the 'towards' emotions of **happiness** (contentment, enjoyment, fun, laughter, joy) to allow us to feel a sense of balance. In **downward spirals** we experience the 'away' emotions of **despair** (depression, hopelessness, confusion) to alert us to the need to restore balance in our life. Again, balance is the key word. Too much happiness may sound impossible but it can cause problems if we lose touch with reality or become obsessed with achieving happiness. Too much despair can send us into a downward spiral of self-pity and self-imposed isolation.

The problem with happiness is that it is a transient emotion, changing with life's spirals. On my seminars I ask people what they want in their life and the conversation goes something like this:

"What do you want to achieve in your life?"
"I want to be successful."
"What do you mean?"
"I want to do well at my job and earn good money."
"What will this give you?"
"Recognition and wealth."
"Why do you want that?"
"It will make me happy."

So the next question I ask is:

"Do you think it is possible to feel happy all of the time?"

Most people agree that happiness describes how we feel at a particular moment in time. They accept that being happy all of the time is an unrealistic aim, given life's spirals. They also suggest that, whilst people may say that they want to feel happy all the time, what makes life enjoyable is actually our ability to experience a variety of emotions, rather than one fixed state.

Many people see happiness as something that has to be pursued. They assume that when they do not feel happy they must be missing something and set off trying to find it. Yet happiness cannot be found, pursued or bought. You see, the search for happiness is futile. Happiness is the by-product of our life being in balance. The only way to achieve it is to ensure that we balance all of our instincts. When you ask happy people why they are happy they often say they don't really know because they don't dwell on the fact that they are happy. Look closer however, and you will find that the core of their happiness stems from the fact that they are content with:

- Who they are
- Their relationships
- Their work (or purpose)
- The pleasures they enjoy
- Their acceptance of uncertainty
- Their appreciation and enjoyment of life

The secret to balancing our Harmony Instinct, therefore, is to focus on managing the five instincts we have already discussed for the following reasons:

- When we balance our Survival instinct we fear nothing and feel comfortable in our own skin because we know and uphold our true values and virtues
- When we balance our engagement instinct we create two way relationships, benefitting from a sense of giving as well as receiving
- When we balance our achievement instinct we fulfil our potential, do our best and feel proud of our achievements
- When we balance our reward instinct we enjoy the pleasures life has to offer without feeling addicted to them
- When we balance our control instinct we stop demanding that the world meets our expectations and relax

When those five instincts are in balance, happiness comes naturally, not because we are searching for it but because we experience the natural sense of inner **Peace** to which the Dalai Lama referred.

Peace

To maintain a sense of inner **peace** we can focus on the **LAUGH** principles:

L ive in the present
A NALyse less
U ncertainty
G ratitude
H umility

So, let's briefly consider the **LAUGH principles** here.

Live in the present

Earlier, when we looked at balancing our Survival Instinct, we saw the importance of putting the past behind us. That though, is only one side of the coin. In order to balance our Harmony Instinct and find happiness, we need to live in the present.

Many of the people who ask for my help come to me believing that they are living in the present, yet all of their energy, focus and talk is about the past or the future. When I observe this and explain that the only place where happiness exists is in the present, many experience a light bulb moment. Understanding that you cannot change whether you were happy yesterday (or not) and you cannot do anything today that will guarantee your happiness tomorrow, opens a window.

The fact is that happiness is how you feel, or don't feel, **NOW** in this particular moment. Living in the present, therefore, is an essential step towards enjoying happiness, because if your mind is elsewhere you cannot hope to be aware of how you feel right now.

A phrase that has become particularly popular in recent years is 'multi-tasking', something it is alleged women do better than men. Undoubtedly we all need to be able to multi task because in our modern world we are invariably called upon to do more than one thing at a time. A mother, for example, is often cooking the tea, talking to her children, watching the television, answering the phone or a knock at the door - all simultaneously. A receptionist at work answers the phone, gives directions to visitors, puts people on hold and issues security badges, often all at the same time. The danger though, is that we continue this approach through the whole of our life, resulting in our life becoming a seamless series of events. If we are not careful, life quickly becomes a treadmill that gets faster and faster. One task merges into another, one day into the next and before you know where you are, your 'bit in the middle' has moved on so fast that you fail to even notice it, let alone enjoy it.

To live in the present we need to slow down and focus on what is right in front of us. How many times have you heard people say, "I've never seen that before" when they enter their office or home after a prolonged absence? And how many times have you spoken to someone who is clearly mentally somewhere else? The fact is that many people today live on autopilot, failing to see what is right under their nose, and that includes people as well as things. Indeed, one of the recommendations made by the Department of Positive Psychology at Harvard University, following extensive research into the concept of happiness, is achieving simplicity. On occasions we need to stand back and simplify our lives. De-cluttering the desk, prioritising our activities, focussing on what really matters, getting rid of the "stuff" we allow to clutter up our lives every day and freeing ourselves from the idea that being busy is an essential part of being human, can help us to dramatically improve our happiness.

One of the reasons people tolerate all of this is the overwhelming tendency to accept compulsion. People often say

"I've got to", "I have to", "I must", "I can't", "I should", "I shouldn't", "I don't have a choice", "It's not up to me" and so on, without even thinking about it. Now, obviously, there are times when such expressions may be true. After all, if you are at work there are certain things you can and cannot do. But I encourage you to rephrase such statements in the future by inserting "I choose to ...." in front of your intended action. In this way your response becomes, "I choose to work late", or "I choose to turn up late," and so on. What this does is force you to accept ownership of your life and question whether your lack of choice on occasions is real or self-imposed.

Presence is a timely call for us to pay attention to being and feeling alive. A reminder to stop taking time, people and our life for granted and to pay attention to what we are doing now, in each and every moment. In work, people often talk to each other, but without really paying attention. At home, partners come together, but get wrapped up in "stuff", only often half listening whilst doing something else like watching the television. People bring work home with a thousand excuses regarding why it could not be done in the day. Children struggle in vain to get their parents attention and genuine interest. Modern computer games, and internet surfing have created solitary pastimes which stop families communicating. Sometimes we need to recognise these trends and encourage ourselves and our children to stop what we are doing and talk.

Another important aspect of living in the present is taking time out from our busy lives to have fun. When we were young we searched for fun every day. In the morning we would start and finish a World War and in the afternoon we would win the World Cup or play Hide and Seek. But, as we discussed earlier, the rational part of our brain grows during puberty and one of the side affects is that some adults fall into the trap of taking a much more serious and considered approach to life. In many respects this is good, preparing us for the adult world, but on the other hand we can leave behind so much of what people call our 'inner child'. For some adults life is too serious and should be more fun, otherwise what's the point?

I started this book by suggesting that life is simple and that our primary purpose should be enjoying our 'bit in the middle'. To achieve that we sometimes need to put time aside therefore to make ourselves have fun.

Yes you read that right.

Make ourselves have fun.

Too many people come up with all sorts of excuses for why they can't have fun, but these are simply that, excuses. Fun does not have to be playing games. It can be sharing observations or brief conversations with people, or taking time out at lunchtime to read a book or go for a walk. It can be eating your lunch whilst listening to your favourite music or watching television. At home it can be forcing yourself to spend time playing with your children (whether you feel like it or not), rather than telling them you are too busy. It can be taking your partner for a meal, having a drink with friends or going to the pictures. It can even be having a long soak in the bath. The sources of fun are endless, but sometimes we have to force ourselves to overcome the DART voices that tell us we can't have fun or that we are "busy". Once we do something fun, no matter how reluctantly we may start it, it's amazing how quickly our mood changes. As the old saying goes,

"We don't stop playing because we grow old, we grow old because we stop playing."

To maintain a sense of inner peace we can work on being 'present' and enjoying our lives rather than being passive observers focused on daily routines.

ANALyse less

Many people hinder their chances of experiencing happiness by thinking too much. As a result they suffer from the rational overwhelm we discussed in Part 1. Some of my clients have had such active minds that they felt they could not stop their self-talk. They spent nearly all of their time thinking about and ANALysing everything. This condition does not get nearly as much press as emotional problems like panic or anxiety attacks, but rational overwhelm can be equally disturbing and just as debilitating. It can also be extremely tiring, as the brain rarely rests.

To tackle this problem we need to stop ANALysing things and learn to stop thinking. I know that that sounds easy and it isn't. But thinking is something we take for granted and we rarely question how and when we do it. But it is a habit and, like all habits, it can be stopped. To reduce internal self-talk, or constant thinking, practice the 'stop thinking' techniques we discussed in Part 1.

To maintain a sense of inner peace we can practice not thinking and learn to stop trying to ANALyse everything.

Uncertainty

Our world is constantly changing. A key requirement of Emotional Fitness therefore is that we change with it, adapting as we go, rather than standing in the face of the Tsunami of change denying its existence. To practice Emotional Fitness we need to learn to love uncertainty. Deepak Chopra in his book *The Seven Spiritual Laws of Success* puts this best when he says:

"Without uncertainty and the unknown, life is just the stale repetition of outworn memories. You become the victim of the past, and your tormentor today is yourself left over from yesterday."

The search for certainty is a futile attempt to redefine the world according to our individual perception, prejudices, rules, and tolerances. Only by accepting uncertainty do we find the courage to break beyond our self imposed barriers and embrace the risks involved in personal change.

Uncertainty, on the face of it, seems to undermine the whole idea of security. After all, how can we feel secure if we are uncertain. But in that paradox lies the secret to life. By recognising that nothing in our world is certain and that we cannot actually control anything, except our own behaviour, we free ourselves from the futile burden of trying to make everything in our life comply with our expectations. Once we accept that we cannot guarantee what happens in life we cope much better when things go wrong because we do not take the outcome personally. Loving uncertainty makes dealing with life's downward spirals much easier because we accept them, rather than fight or deny them, focusing our attention on what we can do, rather than how offended we are that our rules or expectations have not been met.

The beauty of uncertainty is that it can help us in the battle against fear because if nothing is certain then what is there to be afraid of?

To maintain a sense of inner peace learn to accept uncertainty. I recommend reading the Deepak Chopra quote (above) at the start of every day.

Gratitude

If I have tried to stress one thing in this book above all else, it is that Emotional Fitness represents the ability to choose how you think and feel. This is the ultimate key to achieving happiness. Nothing in this book, or any other book for that matter, can force you to change, that is a choice only you can make.

You can choose to think well of yourself, or live a life plagued with self-doubt. You can choose to build positive relationships, or avoid others or rely on them so heavily that they exploit you. You can choose to fulfil your potential, or throw it all away. You can choose to spend the whole of your life seeking short-term pleasure, or you can master self-discipline. You can choose to spend your life trying to get the whole world to conform to your way of thinking, or you can learn to love uncertainty and diversity. You can choose to love and appreciate the life you have, or you can sit in despair and bemoan lost opportunities and the bad hand you have been dealt.

These are the options that life's spirals throw at us. The choices we make though, are not down to spirals. They are down to the respect we have for ourselves and our own sense of self. For me, life is not about winning or losing. It's about what my daughter called "getting on with it". So I encourage you to express gratitude for the fact that you are alive and appreciate what you have, rather than focusing on what you don't have.

One simple way to do this is to start each day with a simple mantra I call the ABC principle:

> Awake
> Breathe
> Celebrate

Personally I don't know whether there is an afterlife or not. Frankly, I don't think that such matters should dictate our behaviour anyway. My view is that we should strive to maintain high personal standards including honesty, integrity and respect for life and other people because these are the right values for an Emotionally Fit society, not because we stand a chance of qualifying for eternal reward. If we wake each day grateful for the fact that we are breathing and celebrate the opportunity to try to do better today than we did yesterday, then what else is there? If everyone saw life as something to be grateful for we would treat it with far more respect and the world would be better for it.

To maintain a sense of inner peace you can be grateful for what you have, rather than focused on what you don't have.

Humility

You may wonder why I cite humility as the last of the LAUGH principles. The simple reason is that, without humility, life can become no more than a selfish search for self gratification. So what is humility and why is it so important ?

Humility is interpreted by many as the adoption of submissiveness, a lowering if you like of one's own self importance. Such an interpretation however poses a dilemma. How can we have a positive sense of self which promotes confidence and feelings of self worth and yet at the same time practice submissiveness ? For me, the answer lies in understanding the difference between appreciation and importance.

Developing a positive sense of self requires an appreciation of our true values and virtues. That appreciation promotes feelings of self confidence and self worth because we learn to love and accept who we are and the talents we possess. Self appreciation protects our survival instinct because, comfortable with ourselves, we do not feel threatened by external events. This allows us to live in accordance with our values and virtues which in turn ensures that the emotional part of our brain does not experience the sort of internal conflict we discussed earlier. If our self appreciation turns into a sense of self importance however, we become political and competitive because our sense of self becomes based, not upon appreciation of who we are, but upon how we compare with others.

One of the dangers of building a positive sense of self therefore is that we can become self obsessed. I have met many people who have possessed strong self belief and self confidence, but at the same time demonstrated a total lack of humility. Many have been charitable donors, to their great credit, but were unaware of their constant self focus. They often saw themselves as being right, talked about themselves all the time and maintained a closed rather than open mind, seeking to persuade others to their view or impress others with their knowledge or skills. This type of confidence can quickly turn into arrogance which makes people un-teachable because their sense of self is based on their own importance.

Most religions recognise this potential human failing and tackle it by promoting the love of something more important than ourselves, namely God (the exact nature of God depending upon the religion), and the need to love and serve others. Such beliefs provide a positive guide to anyone wishing to avoid the dangers of self interest because they encourage believers to accept submission to a higher authority or greater cause. But even spiritual beliefs can fall victim to self interest. When believers focus on the politics of their brand of religion rather than practicing its virtues, they can become defensive or aggressive, seeking to protect rather than accept challenge to their beliefs. Many of today's world conflicts are religiously motivated in this way because believers have fallen into the trap of ego driven self interest rather than humility. Some even choose to re-interpret the true spiritual message in their religion to justify their aggressive actions. Whether we accept the existence of God or not is a matter of personal choice. The important point is that without humility we will always remain vulnerable to self interest driven by ego. Only when we learn to surrender this can we truly hope to find lasting happiness.

The human need to feel important is part of our natural instincts and we cannot just delete it. What we can do however is change how we define that importance. We cannot achieve lasting happiness if we measure our importance in terms of status, wealth, territory, possessions or accolades. These are the trophies of ego driven self importance. The only route to lasting happiness lies in measuring our importance in terms of how much we **positively** affect the hearts and minds of the people we come into contact with during our life. These are the trophies of self unimportance, in other words, humility. I therefore recommend humility as the final part of *Emotional Fitness* because, without it, everything is self interest. Selfish self interest lies at the heart of all human conflict. Master humility and we end human self destruction for ever.

Self appreciation is a virtue because underpins our positive sense of self but self importance based on ego is a vice which keeps us locked in the "survival of the fittest" mentality which still holds the human race captive. Overcoming this last bastion of our animal conditioning is, I believe, the biggest battle facing our race and the biggest obstacle to the world achieving Emotional Fitness.

I started this book by quoting my daughters expression regarding the simplicity of life. It is only fitting therefore that I should conclude this part of the book with another of her expressions, which she regularly quotes to me, and which seems most appropriate here ;

"**Dad, get over yourself** "

If a clearer definition of humility exists, I haven't seen it.

To maintain a sense of inner peace and lasting happiness we can embrace humility by valuing our sense of self, but without becoming obsessed with our own importance.

Peace workouts

If you want to measure how balanced your Harmony Instinct is, why not complete our online Emotional Fitness questionnaire which you will find on our web site **www.emotionalfitnessgym. co.uk** .

In the meantime, to develop a sense of PEACE in your life and put the principles we have discussed into practice, why not follow the workouts provided below.

1. Live in the present

- Identify 3 things you can do to slow down and live more in the present.
- Identify 3 things you can do to plan your time better so that you take time out from work.
- Identify 3 ways you can build more fun into your life.
- Identify 3 ways you can appreciate your life and the people in it more.

2. Stop / Start guide

Below you will find a few more ideas regarding things you can STOP or START doing in order to develop a sense of PEACE in your life. I recommend you select one idea from each list and practice them both for 24 hours. Then select another 2 ideas and so on to suit your particular needs.

STOP

1. Rushing around and saying how "busy" you are.
2. Cramming too many things into your day with no space.
3. ANALysing everything you do (and yourself).
4. Telling yourself you have no choices. Avoid saying "got to", "have to" etc.
5. Thinking about the past and the future all of the time. Focus on NOW.

START

1. Expressing gratitude for your life at the start and end of every day ("ABC - Awake / Breathe / Celebrate.")
2. Practicing either of the 'stop thinking' exercises in Part1 (workouts 7 & 8) daily.
3. Planning fun activities into your life.
4. Enjoying uncertainty by smiling when things go wrong before taking action.
5. Practicing humility by :
   a. Listening first in your conversations with others
   b. Leading with questions NOT your views
   c. Showing genuine interest in other people

Chapter 2.8: Summary

Life, as my daughter suggested, is a simple proposition, made simpler by choosing to enjoy it. Choosing though, involves a relationship between the emotional and rational parts of our brain. Managing that relationship is the key to achieving Emotional Fitness which itself is the real secret to achieving lasting happiness.

Emotional Fitness is a call for us to wake up to the fact that we are not what we feel and think. The physical feelings, emotions and thoughts that we experience everyday are the by-product of our brain's instinctive ability to recognise our needs and motivate us to satisfy them. This is an ancient process and one which reacts so fast that it bypasses our conscious ability to choose. Emotional Fitness is all about taking back control of this process.

Understanding the purpose of our instincts, the emotions they use to guide us, and the impact they have on our thinking, is critical if we are to recognise the signs and stop ourselves becoming victims of emotional and rational overload. In this book I have highlighted the six **SEARCH** instincts that have the most profound impact on our mental health, the emotions they use to guide us towards and away from things, how they affect how we think and feel and the six principles we can focus on to develop an Emotionally Fit mind:

Perspective

We can only achieve lasting happiness if we first love who we are and the life we are given.

People

We can only achieve lasting happiness if we share our love with others and avoid dependency and exploitation.

Purpose

We can only achieve lasting happiness if we fulfill our potential and to achieve that we need to rationally and emotionally believe in ourselves and our ability to succeed.

Pleasure

We can only achieve lasting happiness if we control our basic desires and demonstrate self restraint.

Power

We can only achieve lasting happiness if we control ourselves rather than trying to control other people.

Peace

We can only achieve lasting happiness if we take time out to appreciate being alive, stop allowing thoughts and feelings to dictate who we are and practice humility.

These 6 Ps allow us to satisfy our instinctive needs positively, rather than allowing them to turn us into their slavish victims, driving us into despair and an endless pursuit of short term satisfaction.

Whether you use the principles of Emotional Fitness outlined in this book is a choice that only you can make. I hope that, whatever your decision, you will at least take ownership of how you feel and think in the future and not allow anyone or anything to steal that right from you. Hopefully the summary in Table 3 will help you to remember the key principles we have discussed.

And don't forget

To measure how balanced your SEARCH instincts are, and to track your progress in improving your Emotional Fitness, you can complete the online Emotional Fitness questionnaire on our web site at www.emotionalfitnessgym.co.uk .

SEARCH instincts	The 6 Ps	The principles	The benefits
Survival Purpose - physical + psychological	PERSPECTIVE	**S** elf talk (**DART v COPE**) **E** motional control (**RADAR**) **L** et go of the past (**CLEAR**) **F** ind your true sense of self (**values & virtues**)	A positive sense of self Greater self confidence
Engagement Purpose - breeding & connection	PEOPLE	**E** xpectation **E** xchange **E** quality **E** mpathy **E** ncouragement **E** xpression **E** njoyment	Positive two way relationships Greater sense of loving and sharing
Achievement Purpose - self fulfilment	PURPOSE	**B** rutal reality (face it) **O** ptimism (maintain it) **B** ias for action (do it)	A clear purpose in life Less procrastination - more action Achieve your goals
Reward Purpose - satisfaction of needs	PLEASURE	**I** dentify habits **D** eclare war **E** nvironment (change it) **A** lternatives (find some) **L** ive your values	Greater self discipline Addiction avoidance
Control Purpose - security	POWER	**R** ules **E** xpectations **A** nger **C** ommunication **T** olerance	Reduced anger and frustration More positive support of others
Harmony Purpose - Balance & well being	PEACE	**L** ive in the present **A** nalyse less **U** ncertainty **G** ratitude **H** .umility	Greater appreciation of being alive More fun

Table 3

The SEARCH summarised

Part 3: The Proof

This section of the book presents a collection of Emotional Fitness success stories.

These success stories are included to show you real life examples of how Emotional Fitness problems can wreak havoc in people's lives and how the principles outlined in this book can make a real difference.

The stories are based on real life people but the names, identities and, in some cases, gender, have been changed to protect their privacy. Some of the details have also been adapted for the same reason.

The essence of their stories, however, is based on real life.

Chapter 3.1: A Survival success story

Roger

Roger was abandoned into an orphanage at the age of five by his parents. Being of mixed race, he stood out and other children were quick to pick up on and make fun of his 'differences'. Subjected to continuous verbal abuse and physical attacks from other children, singled out for blame when things went wrong by the people who ran the orphanage, his life became a misery.

Roger first approached me in his mid forties. He complained that he had two voices in his head, which prevented him from making decisions. He explained that in business negotiations he heard one voice in his head saying "Go for it", and another, different voice, saying "Don't trust them". Now, we have already established that the rational part of our brain likes two sides of an argument, but the problem was that the emotional part of Roger's brain would not let him make a decision.

During our time together Roger recalled his brutal childhood experiences. He cried out at one stage in a childlike voice, "I'll never let anyone get close to me again". This strategy, borne out of tragic circumstances, became a permanent part of Roger's 'sense of self'. Unable to accept himself for who he really was, because that person was constantly being brutalised, Roger became someone else. He learned to trust nobody, keeping everybody at arm's length to protect himself. He married three times, all three relationships ending in divorce as he rejected anyone's attempts to get beneath his protective shield.

He became an incredible comedian and mimic. Everyone who knew him saw him as the life and soul of any party. Deep down though, Roger was unhappy. In his business meetings he wanted to be himself and do what was right, but he remained haunted by the cries of a child warning him of the dangers of trust.

Roger lived his life protecting a false sense of self. The voices in his head were those of an adult wanting to embrace life and a child who trusted no one. Once he recognised that one of the voices in his head was merely an 'echo' from his past and that the **DART** strategy he had developed as a child to protect himself was no longer appropriate in his adult life, he made an incredible and rapid transformation. Roger's **Survival Instinct** was on high alert. He had a low sense of self and saw the outside world as a threat, even though he wanted to exploit its opportunities.

Working with Roger involved balancing his **Survival Instinct** through embracing the **Perspective principles**. To start with we used the guided meditation included in Part 1 to help him put the past behind him and recognise his true potential. He reviewed his sense of self by exploring his real values and virtues, which helped him to start believing in himself again. He learned to stop the negative **DART** self-talk that had dominated his life and chose to replace it with **COPE** self-talk, which focused his attention on his options and what he could do rather than what he couldn't. He began making decisions based upon what he wanted, rather than the echoes of his childhood. Once he balanced his **Survival Instinct** he also used the **7 Es of Engagement** to re-look at his marriage and began to balance his **Engagement Instinct** by focusing on what he could put into his marriage rather than seeing it as somewhere to hide.

Roger went from strength to strength.

The day following our work together, Roger sent me a text I will never forget:

"Paul thank you for your help yesterday. This morning I woke up and looked in the mirror and for the first time in my life only one pair of eyes looked back."

As Roger realised, our sense of self can easily become defined by echoes from our past, which trigger our **Survival Instinct** and emotions of fear, which, in turn, lock us into negative thinking. But the past is not who we are, anymore than our thoughts and feelings are who we are. We are so much more than all of these things. Too often we allow the echoes of our past to haunt us, diminishing our belief in our strengths, talents and abilities, personal values and potential.

Chapter 3.2: An Engagement success story

Simon

Simon struggled in his relationships. No sooner would he establish a loving relationship than he would resort to self-destructive behaviour. Once any of his relationships went beyond the original novelty, he would begin complaining about minor things, would embarrass his partner in public when they went out with friends by picking arguments, getting blind drunk and causing a scene. He would become terribly possessive and jealous of his partner, constantly checking their phone and whereabouts. Small arguments would be blown out of all proportion and he would begin to blame his partner for everything that went wrong.

In working with Simon it became clear that from an early age he had craved the attention and approval of his father, which had never been forthcoming, or at least not to Simon's satisfaction. Constantly negatively compared to his brother, and feeling like a failure, Simon resorted, subconsciously, to **DART** thinking, which encouraged him to get attention any way he could. Before long Simon won that attention by behaving in destructive ways that constantly got him into trouble. Soon Simon's sense of self developed into that of a drama maker. His life became a series of successes followed by failures, his business activities ranging from rapid success to bankruptcy. The hurt of early rejection had clearly adversely affected Simon's ability to engage successfully.

His self-destructive behaviour was designed to exploit the empathy of those who cared about him, but for Simon their love was no more than the affection of an audience he had always been seeking.

Following the principles of Emotional Fitness Simon first used the survival **SELF** principles to find his true sense of self by questioning his true values and virtues and put the past behind him. He recognised that his relationships in the past were based on his need to be loved, rather than on giving love. He developed a plan to review with his girlfriend whether their relationship was working for both of them and, using the **7 Es of Engagement,** he began to focus on what he could put into the relationship, rather than what he was getting out of it.

This new focus helped him to feel better about himself and also benefited his **Achievement Instinct** because, free from the dramas of relationship crises, he was able to refocus on what he wanted from his work.

Ultimately, Simon re-balanced his life, built a much stronger relationship with his girlfriend and experienced much greater happiness and positive self-esteem by rejecting a life built on the selfish exploitation of others for personal gain.

Chapter 3.3: An Achievement success story

Charles

Charles had always wanted the love and affection of his parents. He rarely got it. He was regularly criticised by them and felt that he could do nothing right. Initially, Charles tried hard to impress them. Finding that no matter what he did, he never got the recognition that he so desperately craved, Charles eventually gave up. **Apathy** became Charles' default emotion. "What's the point?" became his self-talk.

During one school sports day, for example, Charles found himself competing neck and neck with another boy in a race, but his parents could not attend the event and so, just yards, from the finishing line, Charles stopped running, letting his friend win. After all "What was the point?"

Over time Charles came to define himself by this sense of **apathy**. After all, "If no one cares", he thought, "then there's no point trying". He even carried that mantra into adulthood, always achieving the bare minimum he needed to achieve in order to get by. Everyone used to tell Charles that he was capable of achieving so much more. This meant little to him though, because he had decided that achieving was a waste of time. When Charles did earn spare money he spent it all on accumulating things he didn't need, after all, "No point saving", he thought. Eventually he began spending on anything that would give him short-term pleasure.

Using the **SELF and BOB principles** of Emotional Fitness, Charles eventually learned to face the brutal reality of what he was doing. He used the **SELF** principles to let go of the childhood tape that was constantly running in his head and defined his true values. He came to realise that the only person he was short-changing was himself. Once he restored a more positive sense of self he was able to tackle the **apathy** that had been the centre of his life for so long.

Using the **Achievement** workout in Part 2, Charles worked out his strengths and what he enjoyed doing. He began to research job opportunities that allowed him to exploit his strengths, took action by applying for those jobs and eventually forged a successful career doing something that he loved. Occasionally Charles would report that the **DART** voices of procrastination had returned, but he had learned how to ignore them and refused to let them dictate how he was thinking and feeling.

Chapter 3.4: A Reward success story

Helen

Helen came to see me because she was feeling depressed and struggling with her weight. During our conversation it appeared that Helen had always had a difficult relationship with her mother, as result of which her teenage years were dominated by constant rows at home. Helen recalled how, at the age of 16, after one such row, she fled to the kitchen and began eating. This action gave her a sense of calm and comfort. Innocent enough perhaps, yet before long, this pattern of eating for comfort became a way of life.

As Helen reflected on her life, she realised that, whenever she felt emotionally uncomfortable or stressed, she would always feel compelled to turn to food for comfort. Helen constantly talked about going on diets, and in fact did manage to lose weight on occasion, normally when she had a specific goal, like losing two dress sizes because she was going on holiday. Despite her best efforts though, she would always return to over-eating whenever life got tough.

Helen's eating habits followed a similar daily pattern. Often skipping breakfast, she would eat little during the day, which she rationalised as helping her to lose weight, only to experience 'starving' feelings when she got home. As a result, Helen would tuck in to high carbohydrate foods to overcome the feeling of starvation. Shortly afterwards she would feel guilty and eat again to comfort herself, rationalising that she could start dieting again tomorrow.

Throughout this pattern of behaviour, Helen was never in control of how she thought or felt. On further investigation it transpired that she was frustrated in her relationship with her husband and had never stood up for herself, always putting other people, especially her family, first. This caused her great stress and at times even self-loathing. This in turn led to her feeling trapped.

Helen began by using the **SELF** principles to define her values and virtues and began to realise that she had a right to a life as well as everyone else. She set about re-building her sense of self and, using the **7 Es of Engagement** as her guide, began to stand up for herself, saying "No" when people's demands on her were unreasonable.

Finally, Helen followed the **IDEAL** principles to re-balance her **Reward Instinct**. Rather than following a classic dieting pattern, Helen ate every two hours. She always chose fruit, or a healthy sandwich as an alternative to the comfort food with which she was so familiar. By changing the timing of her eating and by eating small amounts of food every two hours, even when she WASN'T hungry, Helen arrived home after work without the feelings of starvation. Helen also changed her environment, re-arranging her kitchen to put the snack foods out of sight and out of reach. By focusing on what she could eat and by conditioning her brain to know that food was coming regularly, Helen averted the emotional upheaval that she had been experiencing.

Within three months, Helen lost two stone. Most important of all though, Helen felt better about herself and was able to sustain healthier eating habits.

Chapter 3.5: Control success stories

Carl

Carl worked in a highly pressurised environment. As the company he worked for expanded, the pressure he was under at work increased to the point where he felt he was losing control. At the same time his personal life began falling apart. His marriage failed in bitter circumstances and he faced endless problems and arguments regarding access rights to his children.

Carl was a sensitive individual with a strong control instinct. He liked things done properly and had clear views on what people should and shouldn't do and how things should be done. The combination of work and domestic problems led Carl to a place, mentally, where nothing seemed within his control. As a result of this downward spiral, Carl began to impose control. Not on others, though, because they would not listen. Carl imposed control on himself.

He began to spend more and more time on his own, away from people. He locked himself away for hours playing games on the Internet, because that was a world he could control. With no one to criticise or challenge him, Carl felt that, at last, he had restored control in his life. Unfortunately, Carl began to withdraw from reality, to the point where he was medically diagnosed as depressed. He spent several months off work. His control instinct was actually hurting, rather than helping him.

After working with Carl he slowly began to use Emotional Fitness techniques to regain greater balance of his **Control Instinct**. Using the **REACT** principles he began to take small steps, which started with focusing on the things he could control, rather than those he couldn't. He started exercising regularly, which gave him more energy and enthusiasm and spending quality time with his children, when he was with them.

Feeling more in control, Carl soon returned to work and, whilst control was always a part of his life, he learned how to master it, rather than letting it turn into a self-destructive force. Work remained frustrating for him, but he learned to stop moaning about breaches of his rules and expectations. He began to accept that life isn't perfect and stopped taking setbacks and problems personally.

James

James was a businessman who came to see me because he was experiencing regular outbursts of anger, both at work and socially, whenever he felt challenged or frustrated.

Highly competitive, talented and basically a good person, James was hampered by behaviour that, literally, took him over emotionally and dominated his life. During his early years his background left him with little choice but to be bullied or join the bullies. He had chosen to become one of the gang and had learned to get respect from others through intimidation and violence when confronted. This attitude stayed with him, even when playing sports. Now a mature and respectable businessman he found himself applying the same principles that had protected him in his early life. He became angry when people failed or challenged him and his natural **control instinct** led him to wade into issues or people in order to take control of situations, with little concern for the impact he was having on the feelings of others. Often lashing out verbally, and sometimes physically too, James found himself becoming less and less effective at work and less and less happy at home.

Using the **WATCH** principles described in Part 2, James came to realise that he used anger to protect himself by controlling situations, and that his feelings of anger were an instinctive and learned response that could be controlled. He gradually learned to become more sensitive to the motives and feelings of other people. He began to listen, rather than talk, in meetings and he learned not to jump in when things went wrong. Slowly, he began to enjoy 'letting go' and, using the LAUGH principles in Part 2 he targeted his time and energy more positively with his family, friends and colleagues and charity work.

Using the **SELF** principles described in Part 2, James also questioned his true values at work and at home. Gradually, he realised that control may be instinctive, but it can also be destructive when aimed at others. James stopped the negative self-talk that drove him to protect himself by force, and learned that by engaging positively with people, he actually felt better about himself.

Chapter 3.6: A Harmony success story

Sally

Sally felt very unhappy (**Harmony Instinct**). She felt that she had little self-confidence and low self-esteem (**Survival Instinct**). She desperately wanted to be loved (**Engagement Instinct**) and kept trying to achieve this by pleasing people (**Engagement Instinct**). As a result she inevitably attracted the sort of man who treated her badly. She increasingly felt unhappy (**Harmony Instinct**) and drank heavily to try to forget her problems (**Reward Instinct**). As her problems continued, Sally threw herself into her work (**Achievement Instinct**) to avoid having to face her situation. Sally became exhausted and began to suffer from depression (**Harmony Instinct**). She locked herself away from friends and got angry when they challenged her (**Control Instinct**). The imbalance in Sally's instincts was driving a vicious circle built on 'away' emotions, caused by her needs not being satisfied.

Sally's desire to find short-term satisfaction of her needs was getting out of control.

Sally eventually recovered by focusing on the Principles of Emotional Fitness.

- She addressed her **Survival Instinct** using the **SELF** principles (clarifying her personal values and virtues, changing her self-talk, controlling her emotions using the **RADAR** principles, and using the **CLEAR** principles (to put the past behind her.

- She balanced her **Engagement Instinct** by analysing her failed relationships using the **CRASH** model and focused her attention on the **7Es of Engagement**, especially what she could put into her new relationship.
- She recognised that her **Achievement Instinct** was already catered for and, whilst she appreciated that she needed a better work life balance, she realised that she needed to focus on her other instincts.
- She balanced her **Reward Instinct** using the **IDEAL** principles to declare war on the feelings and emotions underpinning her bad habits. She changed her environment by re-arranging her flat. She restricted her alcohol intake to weekends only, and then only in moderation. She found alternatives, joining a gym and working out after work, rather than going home and drinking. She also began choosing better foods to eat.
- She looked at her **Control Instinct** and began using the **REACT** principles, slowly letting go of unimportant things and using her time more effectively, which left her more time to enjoy her life.
- Finally, she balanced her **Harmony Instinct** by following the **LAUGH** principles. She took regular time out each week to enjoy her life. She started each day with a sense of gratitude, dedicated a minimum of 10 minutes at least twice a day to practicing quietening her mind and appreciating what she had in her life and she made sure that she did what she enjoyed doing more often, like visiting the cinema.

Sally now lives with a man in a positive relationship and feels good about her life again.

A poem to conclude

When things go wrong, as they sometimes will,
When the road you're trudging seems all uphill,
When the funds are low and the debts are high,
And you want to smile, but you have to sigh,
When care is pressing you down a bit,
Rest, if you must, but don't you quit.

Life is queer with its twists and turns,
As every one of us sometimes learns,
And many a failure turns about,
When he might have won had he stuck it out;
Don't give up though the pace seems slow
You may succeed with another blow.

Often the goal is nearer than,
It seems to a faint and faltering man,
Often the struggler has given up,
When he might have captured the victor's cup,
And he learned too late when the night slipped down,
How close he was to the golden crown.

Success is failure turned inside out,
The silver tint of the clouds of doubt,
And you never can tell how close you are,
It may be near when it seems so far,
So stick to the fight when you're hardest hit
It's when things seem worst that you must not quit.

Unknown